The Creative Sewing Machine

The Creative Sewing Machine

Anne Coleman

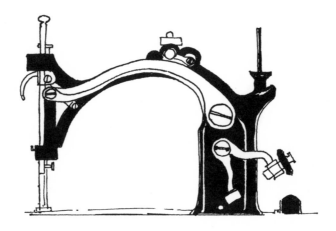

B T Batsford Limited London

© Anne Coleman 1979
First Published 1979
ISBN 0 7134 3309 4

Filmset by Studio 21, Slough, Berks.
Printed in Great Britain by
The Anchor Press Ltd. Tiptree. Essex.
for the publishers BT Batsford Limited
4 Fitzhardinge Street, London W1H OAH

Contents

Acknowledgement

Introduction 7

How a sewing machine
  works 9
The presser foot 9
The feed dog 9
Cams and discs 10
A program 11
Preventing accidents 12
Preparing the machine for
  use 12
The needle 12
The bobbin 13
Machine thread 13
Pinning and tacking 14
Finishing off 14
Taking out 14
Machine types 15

Collecting fabric 16
Sorting and storage 17

Linear patterns and motifs 18
Parallels, angles, zigzags
  and curves 18
Linear or border patterns 19
Motifs 20

Transferring a design 22
Prick and pounce 22
Dressmaker's carbon paper 23
Transparent background 23
Simple designs 23

Enlarging and Reducing 24

Appliqué 25
Reverse appliqué 28

Colour 29
Complementary Colours 31

Patchwork 32
Strips 32
Log cabin patchwork 33
Construction of templates 34

Squares 36
Triangles 36
Diamonds 37

Textures 38
Couching 38
Fringe 39

Block patterns 41

Quilting 41
English quilting 42
Italian quilting 45
Trapunto quilting 46

Shadow patterns
  Wall hanging using
  quilting 48
The quilt 49
The pillow 49
The faces 49

Pleating or tucking 50

Using textures to make a
  wall hanging 52

The zigzag machine 54
Making patterns 55
Fabric appliqué using a
  zigzag stitch 57
Reverse appliqué with
  zigzag stitch 58
Cut work with zigzag stitch 60
Couching with zigzag stitch 61

Free embroidery 64
Preparation of the machine 64
Preparation of the
  background fabric 64
The technique 66

Machine embroidery on
  paper-backed fabric —
  Making a butterfly 68

Simple shapes for pictures 70

Looking for ideas for
  pictures 71
Composition 74
The background 77
People in pictures 80

Machine embroidery with
  a ring 82
Circles and spirals in design 83
Embroidered buttons 87
Quilting 88
To make a quilted fish 89
Making faces 91

Cut work 92

Loosely woven fabrics 94
Removing threads 96

Nets 98
Tulle 98
Plastic net 101

Making a circular hanging 103

Covering wire with thread 104

Stiffening fabrics for
  machine embroidery
  with cellulose paste 105

The bobbin 107
Textures using tension
  variations 109

Automatic patterns 111

Circular sewing 113

Suppliers of equipment
  and materials 117

Further reading 118

Index 119

Acknowledgment

I would like to thank all the people who have helped me in the preparation of this book, particularly Alan J. Oates for taking all the black and white photographs and Peter Coleman for taking the colour slides and also giving help and much encouragement.

Thank you to my daughters, Philippa and Caroline, who modelled the clothes.

I would also like to thank Stephen Plummer of Nottingham Handcraft for help and advice, and Viking Husqvarna for the loan of a sewing machine.

Thanks are also due to the following for allowing photographs of their pictures to be reproduced in this book

Joyce and Alan Oates, page 77

Dan and Paddy Dalloway, page 79

Avon County Council, colour plate facing page 96

AC
Bristol, 1979

Introduction

Our society is dominated by machinery. Because of it we have, on the one hand, a very high standard of living, a great deal of leisure, and a longer and more healthy life; on the other hand, the use of machines has contributed to more and more unemployment among both craftsmen and unskilled workers, and has forced us to use up natural resources which can never be replaced. All this has happened progressively more quickly over the past two hundred years, since the Industrial Revolution, and has changed a way of life which existed for centuries, and upon which much of our present culture is still based. People distrust technology, because not only has it changed, but it has also taken charge of our lives. We fear the escalation of new inventions and more and more dangerous machines and we turn for comfort to the traditional handcrafts such as weaving, sculpture, embroidery and gardening.

It is not at all surprising that the use of a sewing machine for a beautiful traditional handcraft, such as embroidery, is often condemned. The sewing machine, however, is here to stay, and stay longer than the machines which use oil and electricity, for it can be driven just as easily and effectively by manpower. Of course, machine embroidery cannot replace hand embroidery, but it can stand beside it as yet another aspect of the use of fabric and thread in creating exciting effects in textiles.

The sewing machine was invented and patented in 1842. It was probably one of the most important inventions of the Industrial Revolution, both in the home and in industry. Before it was invented, garments were sewn and decorated entirely by hand, so it was of particular importance to workers, already working extremely long hours, to be able to buy cheap, ready-made clothes. Later, the sewing machine became the centre of the ready-made clothing industry which was set up in the North of England. For women workers the factory became an important alternative to going into domestic service. It gave them the independence to lead a private life away from work, and although working hours were long and wages low, the clothing industries were some of the first to be protected by trade unions.

In the home it became, and still is, possible to make more

clothes more quickly and cheaply. In Third World countries it is a valuable piece of equipment which can form the basis of a small home industry.

Today, the dressmaker is able to make a garment completely, including sewing on buttons, making buttonholes and turning the hem, with a modern sewing machine. In fact, the reason why an up-to-date machine may look so complicated, is only because it is required to perform such a large selection of dressmaking processes. But it is still basically a simple machine and can be simply used in just the same way as an older machine.

However, it is also possible to create some exciting effects of a more experimental kind, not necessarily for dress, but for wall-hangings, decorations and so on. Using only a straight stitch and an imaginative selection of fabrics and threads, you can create interesting and unusual textures and patterns. In schools, as well as being of practical help in home economics, a sewing machine can also become a valuable addition to an art room, adding another dimension to work done in textiles and embroidery.

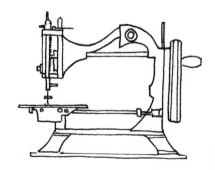

How a sewing machine works

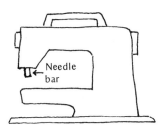

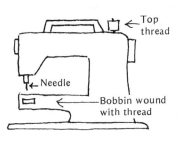

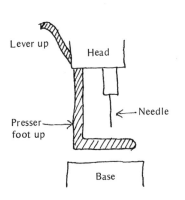

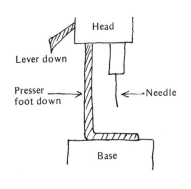

All domestic sewing machines fall into one of three main groups.

1 The straight stitch machine.
2 The zigzag machine.
3 The chain stitch machine.

Both the straight stitch machine and the zigzag machine work on the same basic principle.

The chain stitch machine is different in that it has no bobbin and is not generally used except in toy sewing machines. It gives a pleasant stitch, however, which can be incorporated into a design. Read the manufacturer's instructions, as the thread pulls out very easily and must be properly finished off.

A sewing machine uses two continuous threads to make a line of stitches.

The first comes from a reel of thread which is held in some way above the fabric and goes down through the eye of the needle.

The second thread is wound onto a bobbin which is located somewhere in the base of the machine below the fabric.

The machine needle is held in the needle bar with a screw, and moves up and down vertically. When it moves through the fabric, it enters the base of the machine and locks with the bobbin thread to make a stitch.

The machine needle is moved up and down by power generated by hand, foot (treadle), or electricity.

The presser foot
The fabric to be sewn is held down in position by a presser foot, which is controlled by a lever.

The feed dog
The fabric is moved forward for each stitch by the movement of several rows of little steel teeth, set into the bed or base.

These teeth move every time the needle moves. They are called the feed dog.

In a modern sewing machine they are usually controlled by a button. In older machines, they can be unscrewed and removed.

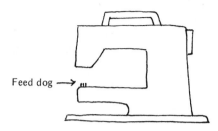

Feed dog →

Before using the sewing machine, look at these things.
1 The top thread holder
2 The needle and needle bar
3 The presser foot and lever
4 The feed dog and control
5 The bobbin in the bobbin case

Up to this point, most sewing machines are similar. However, the zigzag machine, a recent innovation, differs from the straight stitch machine in one important way: it has a needle bar which will move from side to side which enables the machine to make zigzag stitches. This has made the zigzag machine more versatile.

Cams and discs
This method of making zigzag stitches led in turn to the use of cams or discs, which push the needle into stitching a pattern on its journey from side to side.

The cam or disc is precisely cut into a particular shape like an eccentric cog. As it goes round, it acts as a guide and pushes the needle into a different position for each stitch, thus making a pattern, but still keeping within the width of the zigzag made by the needle bar. This is the basis of most push-button sewing machines. Pushing a particular button, or setting a particular program, releases the correct cam into position to make the particular pattern required.

A program
This is a computer term which has been incorporated into sewing machine jargon and means stitch patterns.

It is usually possible to tell the difference between the straight stitch and zigzag machine at a glance. The straight stitch machine has only one disc (for altering the stitch tension) while the zigzag machine has many discs, levers and small diagrams. It is interesting to look at a variety of old and new machines to note the similarities and differences.

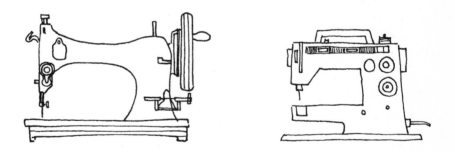

It is possible to buy an attachment which can be used on a straight stitch machine, which pushes the FABRIC from side to side, and thus makes zigzag patterns. Recently, one or two zigzag machines have had this idea incorporated into their design, so that by moving both fabric and needlebar the machine will make much wider zigzag patterns.

Preventing accidents

Using a sewing machine is rather like driving a car. At first, everything seems to be happening at once, but with practice, it becomes easier and eventually quite automatic. However, all machines are dangerous when driven carelessly, and although the sewing machine, is quite safe when used properly, accidents can happen if care is not taken.

To prevent accidents

1 Never put your fingers between the needle and the base.
2 Always take your foot off the controls before changing the needle and threading the machine.
3 If at all possible, use a foot. Even in free embroidery a suitable foot can be used, and this offers some protection to the fingers.
4 Machines should always be switched off and disconnected after use.
5 Machines used by children should always be supervised by an adult.
6 Have the machine serviced regularly.

Preparing the machine for use

Always keep the manufacturer's instructions for reference.

The needle

Machine needles are made in several sizes, so that a suitable needle can be used for a particular fabric. Instruction books usually have a chart of suggested needle sizes. In experimental work, where several fabrics might be used together, use a medium or large needle. If knits or nylon based fabrics are used, try a ball point needle. Special needles can also be purchased to sew leather and suede. If the needle is bent it will not sew evenly, sometimes not at all. Change it carefully and make sure the new needle is screwed right up into the needle bar the right way round.

If the needle is blunt, it will catch the threads of the fabric and pull.

Threading the needle

Following the manufacturer's instructions for your machine, thread the needle. The top thread has to pass through a tension disc which ensures that the top thread is held at the correct tension to sew evenly. If the top tension is too tight, the stitches at the back of the work will be loose. If the top tension is too loose, the stitches on the top of the fabric will be loose. The disc or knob can be twisted to alter the tension. Try this out. Always test the tension on a similar spare piece of fabric before embarking on a piece of work.

The bobbin
Find out how to wind the thread onto the bobbin and make sure that it is evenly wound. Insert the bobbin and position the thread. The tension on the bobbin is altered by a small screw, but this rarely needs to be touched except when carrying out some types of free embroidery (see page 107).

Now the machine is threaded, it is worthwhile double checking to make sure that both needle and bobbin are correctly threaded.

If the machine is not stitching correctly, check the threading first.

Get to know how your sewing machine works by reading the manufacturer's instructions carefully, and practising machining so that your stitching is accurate. Try to drive smoothly, not jerkily, gradually easing up to a higher speed. If the machine is controlled by a foot pedal, it is often easier to keep the heel on the floor and the toe on the pedal.

Machine thread
Machine thread is made from cotton, or polyester. It is best to use cotton only on natural fabrics, but polyester can be used on any fabric, either natural, or synthetic.

Two strands of thread make a more definite top stitch, or it is possible to buy top stitch thread. Machine thread is specially manufactured in plain and shaded colours for machine embroidery. It has a very high lustre and therefore stands out beautifully against the background fabric. Size 30, which is thicker, is much easier to use than 50, which snaps rather easily.

Pinning and tacking

When two or more fabrics are machined together, they should first be pinned and tacked securely together, otherwise the machine will push them out of place. Pins should be placed at right angles to the planned line of stitches, with the points almost touching the line.

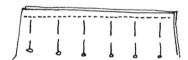

It is then quite safe to machine with the pins in place.

Materials like leather, polythene, suede, PVC, which might show pin marks can be held together with sticky tape.

Finishing off

When the threads of the machining are cut, one remains underneath the fabric, and one on the top. Give the bottom thread a jerk, to pull it through to the back. Tie the ends together.

In free machine embroidery, where there might be a mass of ends, these can be pulled through to the back and trimmed, rather than all tied individually.

Taking out

Where possible, try to avoid taking out stitches, as the marks of the line of stitches show on the fabric. In free embroidery it is often possible to incorporate mistakes in the design.

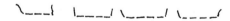

If you must remove stitches, use a stitch ripper and break the line of stitches every 2 or 3 cm.

Pull out the thread between. Always take out from the back of the work.

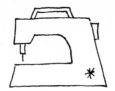

Machine Types

Next to each idea in this book is a diagram of a sewing machine, with one, two, three, or four stars on the base.

Each denotes the type of machine which can be used for the technique described.

★ One star — Any machine. Hand, electric straight, or zigzag. Treadle.

★★ Two stars — Zigzag machine only.

★★★ Three stars — Both hands are needed to control the fabric.
Treadle, electric straight, or zigzag.

★★★★ Four stars — Machine with automatic patterns.

Collecting fabric

When embarking on machine embroidery, it is a good idea to have a varied selection of fabric on which to practise and experiment. Fabric is very versatile, and we use it not only to clothe ourselves, but also to cover and soften our furniture and to decorate our home. Take an interest in the large variety of fabrics which are available. Compare for instance a patterned cotton used for a child's summer dress with the heavy velvet used to cover a chair; the thick tweed of a winter coat and the light chiffon of an evening dress. Notice how people use fabric both in their choice of clothes and in their homes. It is interesting to decide if you like the way in which a particular fabric has been used and why. Do you like the pattern? Is it suitable for a dress or would it look better as a chair cover in a small living room, or perhaps made up into curtains for a large hall? Is the colour just right or is it too bright, too dark or too dull? What about the texture or feel of the fabric? Is it soft and warm, or cold and shiny, or rough and hairy?

Start making a collection of fabrics. Although eventually it is best to built up a large selection, that does not necessarily mean spending a great deal of money. Pieces left-over from dressmaking are useful and dressmaking friends are always willing to hand on pieces of material. A jumble sale in a good neighbourhood can be a treasure trove.

Look out for plain fabrics like linen tablecloths and napkins, plain curtains, plain skirts, cotton dresses with small prints, little-worn satin, brocade, lace evening gowns, chiffon scarves, net curtains. Garments can be used if washed and unpicked. Some shops specialising in upholstery, home-furnishing and lampshade-making often sell bags of superfluous fabrics and short lengths of braid and fringe. Tailors, dressmakers and milliners occasionally sell left-over scraps and sample books. You are lucky to find samples for nothing, but the cost is very little compared with the price you would pay in a shop. Mills offer parcels of fabric pieces by mail order and their advertisements can be found in women's magazines and magazines concerned with embroidery and dressmaking. Street markets all over the country sell short lengths of fabric. Suede and leather pieces are sold by the bag both in markets and leather shops. Do not throw away fruit and vegetable nets, or even bits of plastic netting. Buy as little as 20 cm of fabric; some assistants are more obliging than others! Many people are interested in fabric for various reasons and from them you can hear where the bargains are to be found in your neighbourhood.

Sorting and storage
A collection of fabric can take up quite a lot of space, so be ruthless with pieces that are never used and give them away. With experience, you learn to be discriminating, for some types of fabric do seem to be more useful than others. Keep to one side any pieces of firmly woven fabric which might make a suitable background.

It is easier to manage fabric which has been sorted in some way and many people sort their materials into colour groups, ie reds, blues, yellows, greens, blacks and whites. The following groups are also useful:

1 Small formal prints and patterns like spots, checks, stripes, in cotton and cotton polyester, viscose, fine wool. Cotton prints are useful for patchwork, and the others can be used in appliqué.

2 Plain fabrics like satin, sailcloth, cotton, denim, dupion and other curtain fabrics, trevira, linings and sheeting. These materials are good for stitch experiments, appliqué and quilting. Sheeting can be used for backing and strengthening fabric.

3 Wool, tweeds, suit samples and dress fabrics.

4 Net, tulle, fine nylon, chiffon, organdie, organza, lace, braids, gold lamé, ribbon and fringe.

5 Velvet and corduroy

6 Knitted fabrics like wool jersey, nylon jersey, crimplene.

7 A small selection of large patterned fabric. Some fabric is patterned with distinct motifs which can be cut out and used for appliqué, or quilting.

8 Suede, PVC, polythene and leather.

Sorting is a matter of personal preference.

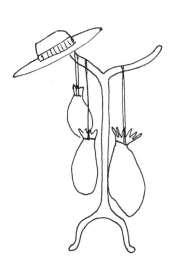

Storage can be difficult for people with little space. Pieces can be stored in shoe boxes, transparent polythene sacks, or even old pillow cases. Drawstring bags can be hung on hooks at the back of a cupboard, behind a door, or under the stairs. Some people iron their pieces and store them in flat boxes under beds, or on top of wardrobes.

Fabric which has been ironed takes up less space.

When working in a carpeted living-space it is a good idea to spread a dust sheet under the whole of the work area. This will catch all the bits of cotton and scraps of fabric, and can easily be taken up, and shaken outside.

17

Linear patterns and motifs

It is not necessary to have a zigzag machine to achieve some striking and useful effects. Many ideas can be carried out on a straight stitch, hand, or treadle, as well as a zigzag machine, and they are all based on what a straight stitch machine is capable of doing. The interest is created by the fabrics and patterns used. A sewing machine makes even stitches in a continuous line. The idea is to see what can be done with a continuous line of stitches to make it more exciting and interesting.

Choose several pieces of firmly woven, medium-weight fabric from your collection, eg trevira, denim, sailcloth, etc. Cut rectangles about 15 cm by 20 cm. Cut on the straight of the fabric. Thread the machine. Use a suitable needle. Check and adjust tension by machining across a scrap of similar fabric. You should always check and adjust tension before beginning to sew. To make a thicker top stitch you can use two threads instead of one.

Parallels, angles, zigzags and curves
Start by making a series of straight, parallel lines down the fabric.

Make them more interesting by placing some close together and some wide apart.

The machine will also make angles. Stitch a short line, then, to make the angle, lift the foot with the needle in the fabric and turn the fabric. Lower the foot and continue to stitch. Make a zigzag line of stitches, then a parallel zigzag line of stitches.

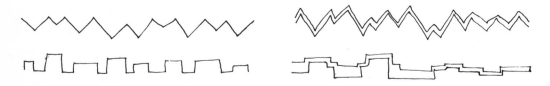

The machine will also make a slight curve.

Stitch and gently move the fabric while stitching. See how tight a curve your machine will make without puckering the fabric. Practise this.

You will see the machine is capable of sewing three sorts of line; straight, curved and angled. How can they be used in design and machining?

Linear or border patterns

A linear pattern is a line of pattern, or a border of pattern. The world abounds in linear patterns and it is interesting to look out for them and even to collect pictures of them to give you ideas for making your own patterns. They are found in border patterns on fabrics and furnishings, on braids, circling round the rims of cups, plates, vases and dishes, and on belts and bracelets. Iron railings make a linear pattern, so do lace, crimps round a pie and patterns in the stone round a church door.

A sewing machine will make both regular and irregular patterns, using the straight lines, curved lines and zigzag lines both separately and together. Try to make some border patterns on a rectangle of fabric. The more patterns you create, the more the quality of the patterns will improve. As you practise, you get into the rhythm of pattern and machine. It is also possible to make similar patterns on paper. If you are not used to drawing, a felt pen is easier to use than a pencil. Hold the pen loosely, and pretend to be doodling. Do a page of patterns, combining zigzags with straight lines, using different angles, superimposing patterns and curves.

Keep both machined and drawn patterns in a folder and try to make a note of other inspiring linear patterns in the environment. Making patterns like this is one of the first steps in design.

Try making designs on striped, checked and spotted fabrics, using the fabric design to enhance the machine stitches. Border designs can also be carried out on ribbons or plain bindings.

1 Line patterns using double top thread

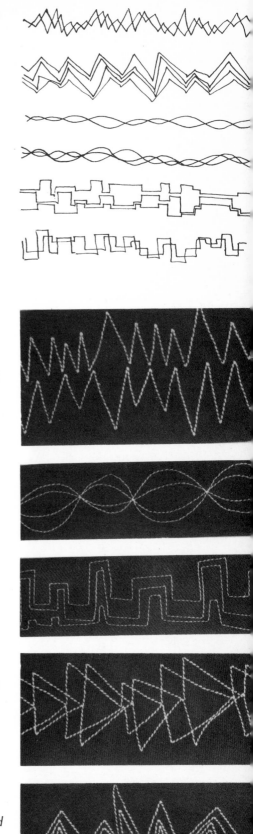

Motifs

Straight, wavy and angled lines which continue along a plane make linear or border patterns, but if a line continues round an area and meets itself again, it will make an isolated shape, or motif.

Making continuous line motifs is easy on a sewing machine if you remember that the machine will go forward, make straight lines, angles and slight curves.

To practise, take a square of fabric about 12 cm and using a piece of sharpened tailor's chalk, draw a rough square about 10 cm on the fabric. Start machining a line from some point on the edge of the chalk square and fill the square with a continuous line, to make a pattern, finishing where you began.

Experiment by making different angles, going in various directions and crossing lines. Try starting the pattern from points within the square, as well as from the edge. After a little practice you will find that you are making more interesting patterns and will have some ideas of the ones you like best.

These sort of patterns can also be drawn with a felt pen on paper. Do not be satisfied with one or two experiments, but keep on doodling both on the machine and with a pen. It sometimes takes several attempts to discover one or two really satisfactory patterns. These can become quite complicated and fascinating.

 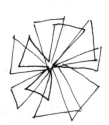  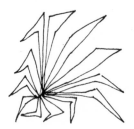

To transfer a design onto fabric to see how it will look when machined, trace it off on tissue paper, pin it to the fabric and machine carefully round the design. Pull the paper away. In this way, it is possible to plan quite complicated patterns on paper and then transfer them to fabric. However, it is also worthwhile doodling with the sewing machine straight onto the fabric. In this way you will get used to the working of the machine and find out what can be achieved.

Isolated motifs are used in decoration on many things. Look out for interesting examples in woodcarving, on fabric, in pottery. Some very formal motifs can be seen on arabian rugs and carpets, in traditional fabric designs, on old enamelled tiles and in carved stonework. However, motifs can also be informal and modern pottery designs are a good example of this.

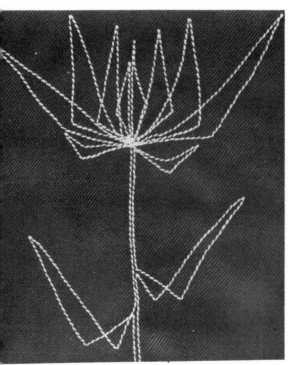

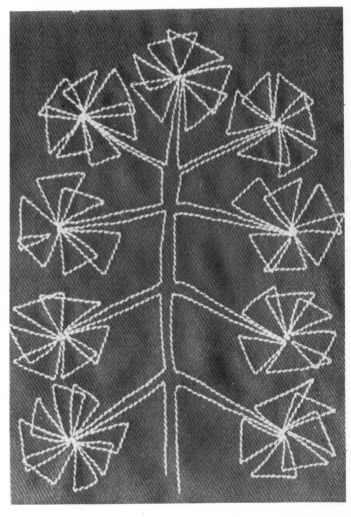

2 and 3 Continuous line motifs, using double top thread

Decorative uses
Both linear patterns and motifs can be used to decorate clothes, accessories and home furnishings. Any embroidery should be done before a garment is cut out. Lay the pattern pieces on the fabric and draw with tailor's chalk round those to be decorated, then machine and press. If you are doing several rows of machined pattern, hold the fabric taut in an embroidery ring. Use border patterns to decorate hems, belts, cuffs, stripes and edges.

It is easy to repeat a few centimetres of linear pattern if you start and finish the design at the same level.

Motifs will decorate collars, yokes, tee shirts, pockets and ties. They can also be used on tablecloths, napkins, cushions and bags.

There are several methods of transferring designs onto fabric. Choose the most suitable.

Transferring a design

1 Prick and pounce. This method of transfer is by far the best, although it takes some time to carry out. It is excellent for very detailed designs and for use on rough or loosely woven fabric.

Trace the design onto tracing paper. Use a hard, sharp pencil for an accurate line.

Place the tracing onto a folded blanket or an ironing board and carefully prick every 3 mm along the lines of the design with a crewel needle.

Turn the tracing over and gently rub the back with fine sandpaper.

This removes the nibs of paper pushed through by the needle. Now the tracing is ready for use.

Pin the tracing onto the fabric, (for leather, etc stick it with tape), make sure it is in the correct position and the right way round. Ensure it is held securely.

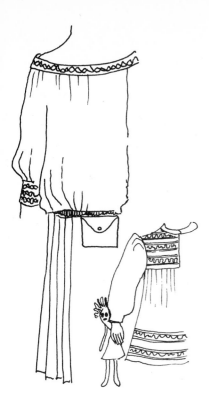

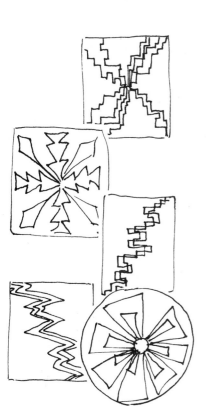

Take a strip of felt, and roll it into a cylinder securing it with a couple of stitches.

With the felt shape, gently rub talc (or pounce if you can get it) all over the design. If the fabric is white or very pale, add a little ground charcoal.

Carefully LIFT the design from the fabric, and you will see the talc has gone through the holes, leaving the design marked out in dots.

Join the dots with a fine brush and white (or pale blue) poster paint.

The design can be used again and again and is also suitable for transferring repeated patterns.

2   Dressmaker's carbon paper is made in various colours. Choose the colour which will show up on the background fabric. Only use carbon paper on smooth fabrics. An uneven surface will make blobs. Place the carbon paper face down onto the fabric. Place the design over the carbon paper. Making sure they are in the correct position, trace over the design, using a sharp pencil or a dressmaker's wheel.

3   Transparent background. It is sometimes possible to trace a design straight onto a background if the fabric happens to be translucent or semi-transparent. Make sure the design shows to best advantage by going over it with waterproof ink or, if the fabric is dark, with white poster paint. Place fabric over design and secure. Trace with a fine brush and poster paint. It is sometimes possible to use this method by putting the design and fabric background against a window, so that the light shines through, showing up the lines of the design. Stick the design and fabric to the window with sticky tape.

4   A very simple design can be transferred by tracing the design onto tracing paper, then tacking the tracing onto the background. Go round the design with small stitches. Tear away the paper.

5   If the design is a simple motif, a tracing can be taken, the design cut out and pinned to the background. Paint round the edge very carefully.

Points to remember
   1 Never cut up or destroy the design. Always trace off a copy to use in transfers.
   2 Never use a biro, soft lead pencil, or felt pen on fabric. They can smudge and the marks are virtually impossible to remove.

It is always worth spending a little extra time to get a really good result.

Enlarging and reducing

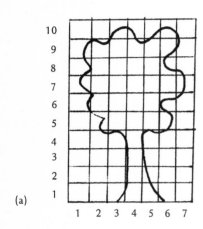

(a)

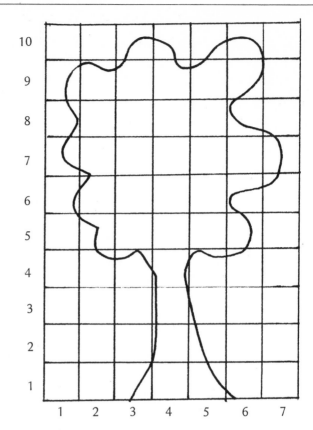

(b)

Enlarging or reducing a sketch, so that it is the size you want for a design is a very useful skill, and quite easy to do.

Take the small sketch and divide it into squares.

Figure (a) divided into 70 squares (10 by 7).

Take a piece of paper the size you intend the finished picture to be.

Divide the paper into the same pattern and number of squares as the small sketch, ie 10 by 7.

Number the squares down the side and across the bottom.

Using a pencil, copy what you see in the small squares into the corresponding large squares.

When you have a satisfactory copy, go over the design in waterproof ink.

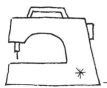

Appliqué

Appliqué means applying fabric shapes to a background and attaching them with stitches.

The technique can be carried out very successfully using a straight stitch machine, if care is taken over the design. Remember that the machine will only do certain things easily, eg, go forward, make a slight curve, make angles. Therefore a design should be chosen with this in mind.

For a person who has little or no experience of creating a design this might seem a daunting task. However, the secret of all design is to start very simply then gradually progress to something more complex.

(a)

A sewing machine can be easily manoevered round a rectangular shape. Almost all buildings are based on rectangular shapes so why not start by making an appliqué picture of a house, your own house or a row of houses? This might be any row of houses, perhaps in the centre of a town, or a row of modern semi-detached houses, a row of terrace houses, or a line of old cottages. You can make a sketch, or take a photograph of the houses and use this as a basis for the design. Photographs are very useful if you cannot draw very well.

(b)

This picture is based on a photograph of a row of houses in a fishing port. A photograph will include people, buildings, cars, posts and poles, wires and aerials and other objects which you will not want to include in your picture. Take a sheet of tracing paper and trace off only the buildings you want to embroider, and only the details, (doors, windows, etc), on the buildings which you want to include. You will then have a tracing with no shadows and no superflous detail (see figure b).

This sketch may be too small, so it has to be enlarged to the size of the finished work (See page 24).

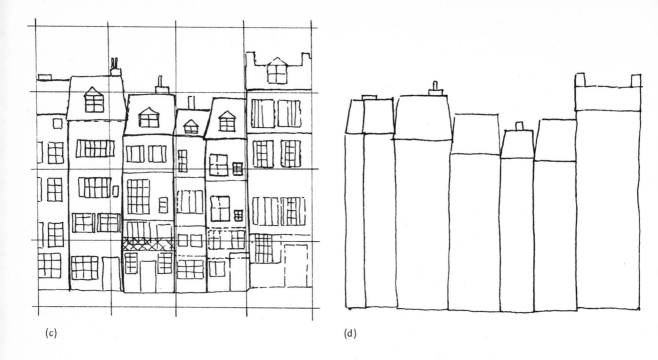

(c)

(d)

When you are enlarging the design you may also have to change the angle of the houses slightly, so that they are flat and lose perspective (see figure c). This simplifies a design and makes it easier to carry out in fabric shapes. Trace off the main shapes of the houses onto a piece of tracing paper (see figure d). These can then be cut out and used as pattern pieces. Choose a firmly woven fabric for the background. This row of houses was stitched onto a poplin background and bonded onto a piece of calico to give more body. However, it could also have been strengthened with a piece of iron-on interfacing. Cut the rectangle of background material on the straight grain of the fabric. Leave a small border round the edge for a turning. Small-print cotton, gingham, stripes, spots and checks are very good for house shapes. Choose colours which look well together. Pin the pattern pieces onto the straight grain of the fabrics and cut out.

Place the fabric shapes onto the background. There is no need to turn in the edges, for a picture is not subject to wear and tear like a garment.

You can either pin and tack, lightly glue with fabric glue, or bond with a bonding web to hold the pieces in position. Carefully sew with the machine using a matching thread.

4 Appliqué picture using simple rectangular shapes

Finally, cut out the doors and windows, using suitable fabrics. When machining fabric shapes onto a background, it is always easier, where possible, to machine from the middle, out to the edge. This stops the fabric from being pushed out of position. For instance, these windows were machined starting right in the middle of each window, going out to the side, then round the edge, and back across the middle.

Press carefully and mount.

It is interesting to cut freehand rectangles of fabric in different sizes and arrange them to make groups of buildings. Choose fabrics which are printed in patterns which will help in the final design.

Always try to use the pattern on the fabric to help you.

Applied fabric shapes can be used on both dress, accessories, and home furnishing, but the edges of the shapes should be turned in and tacked securely before attaching with machine stitches, so that the fabric does not fray out when laundered.

Although the machine will not sew round a small circle, or a tight curve with straight stitch, it is possible to overcome this by making a straight line motif in the middle of a circle which will attach the round fabric shape to the background.

Make use of non-fray fabrics like net, knits, felt, leather, lace, ribbon and suede, or fabrics which can be fringed out attractively at the edge.

Reverse appliqué

This is another technique which can be used to make a motif or appliqué more varied. Three or four layers of non-fray fabric are sandwiched together and backed with a piece of cotton, calico, or firm fabric. The fabrics are tacked firmly together, both round the edge and across the middle, to prevent slipping. The design or pattern is machined. Some parts can then be cut away to reveal the fabric beneath, and colours and patterns should be chosen with this in mind. It is easier to start with felt, but experiment with different non-fray fabrics like net, coloured interfacing and knitted fabrics. Reverse appliqué with straight stitch is not suitable for laundering.

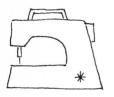

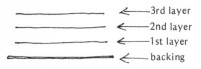

5 Sampler, using three layers of nylon jersey

28

Colour

In design, colour is as important as pattern and shape. Working with fabric is rather like working with paint which has already been mixed into all the tones and hues one could wish for. Since embroidery is partly concerned with using colour, doing one or two experiments with scraps of coloured fabric can be very intriguing and enlightening.

There are three primary colours RED BLUE YELLOW.

The red is a red without any trace of blue or yellow.

The blue has no trace of yellow or red.

The yellow has no trace of red or blue.

See if you can find scraps of primary blue, red, or yellow, in fabric, or thread.

From these three colours, mixed in various proportions, come all the other colours.

An equal proportion of red and yellow make orange.

An equal proportion of blue and yellow make green.

An equal proportion of red and blue make purple.

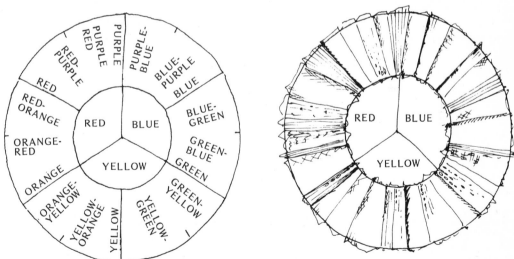

Using this information, it is possible to make a colour circle from fabric scraps. Choose plain fabrics, or plain areas of patterned fabrics and clear tones. A clear tone should not be muddy or dark, or pale and chalky. Cut thin strips (about 1-1.5 cm) and arrange in a circle, placing the fabric so that the strips go from red, through red/orange to yellow, and so on. In reality, colours gradually merge into one another so that it is impossible to see any real line between each. Look at a rainbow, a prism, or oily water to see the spectrum of colour, and the relationship between each.

Keep the fabric circle to help you choose colour schemes.

It soon becomes clear that some tones of a colour can be dark and rather muddy. These *hues* contain a proportion of black. The darker the colour, the higher the proportion of black.

On the other hand, other *tones* of a colour are quite light and pale. These pastel colours have a proportion of white and the lighter the colour, the higher the proportion of white.

Here are a few experiments with colour tones.

1 From your collection of fabric, choose all the possible tones of one colour. Try to arrange these from very pale, through to very dark. Strips can be arranged and stuck. Because these colours are closely related to one another they go together very well. An embroidery carried out in tones of one colour can be very effective and can look very rich.

2 Another experiment showing this grading in colour can be done by collecting together pieces of fabric in shades of grey, right up from dark grey, medium and pale grey and white. Dye these together in a pan, using a small tin of hot water dye, in a light clear colour. (Follow instructions; one tin of dye with one tablespoonful of salt, and water to cover).

3 Using poster paint, take one primary colour, black and white and make a chart of graded colour. Gradually add more and more white to the colour until it grades into all white.

The colour can also be shaded down with black, until it is all black.

Some paint shops have paint mixers and colour charts which show examples of colours very subtly graded from light to dark. Look at the machine to see what colours are used. It takes very few colours to mix hundreds of other tones and hues.

Complementary colours

Every colour has another colour which complements it to best effect. On a colour wheel, this happens to be the colour directly opposite on the circle. Artists and craftsmen use this fact to advantage in painting, fabric printing, etc, but it is most easily seen in magazine layouts, colour advertisements and so on. The complementary colour can be very little, maybe just a spot of colour.

1 From your fabric collection, find several pieces of fabric in tones of the same colour and put a very small piece of contrasting fabric with the group.

2 Find a piece of patterned fabric which makes use of complementary colours.

Become colour conscious when looking at window displays, magazines, and shop layouts and try to analyse the colour schemes used. One should always treat colour very gently and not splash it around indiscriminately. It is not necessary to add complementary colour to every piece of work, but it is interesting to know that it exists and can be used. At first, it is a good idea to use tones of one colour, or a small group of adjacent colours on the colour wheel, then perhaps move onto a more exotic colour scheme as you gain experience. It is possible to create a mood with colour, and it is helpful to use words to describe the colour mood of a fabric.

hot	exciting	dark
warm	calming	light
cool	reassuring	bright
cold	frightening	dull

Find a piece of fabric, patterned or plain, which could be described by each word.

Find groups of fabrics which could be described by a word from two or three of the columns, eg hot, exciting and dark, or cool, light and calming.

Become aware of colour in the environment and notice how mood is created by colour, in colour TV and at the cinema. Experiment with colour in embroidery, so that you become able to use it to create the effect you desire.

6 Motifs can be used to decorate clothes. Free machine embroidery on applied fabric shape

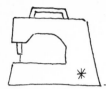

Patchwork

Patchwork is the sewing together of geometric shapes cut from fabric. The shapes must be accurate so that they fit in with each other to form an all-over mosaic pattern.

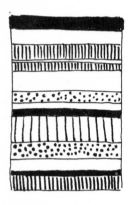

Patchwork is normally associated with hand embroidery, but several shapes are suitable for use with a machine. These are shapes which can be sewn together to make a strip, then the strips can, in turn, be sewn together to make a piece of fabric.

Patchwork can be used for home furnishings like cushions and bedspreads, as well as for clothes and accessories.

Well-made and accurate templates can be purchased at haberdashers, craft shops and chain stores, but if these happen to be the wrong size, it is possible to construct a template with a pair of compasses, ruler and set square. This must be done carefully because, if a template is inaccurate, the piece of work will go progressively wrong.

Always use the same type of fabric throughout one piece of work. Cotton, cotton polyester, velvet, silk, corduroy are all suitable for patchwork. Never use knitted fabrics or anything loose-woven and stretchy.

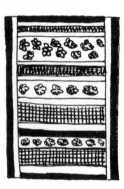

Strips
One of the easiest ways of making a patchwork is to join strips of fabric. It is important always to cut the strips on the straight grain of the fabric so that each strip is the same width all the way along. To machine, pin baste with pins set at right angles to the seam line with the point of the pins just below the seam line.

The edge of the machine foot against the edge of the fabric will give a suitable seam allowance and is easier to follow than a drawn line.

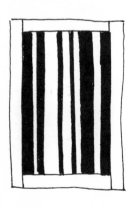

Sewing strips of fabric like this is very easy, but by choosing interesting combinations of colours and patterns and by varying the width of the strips, it is possible to create some lovely effects. Choose the position of each colour, before beginning.

When the strips are sewn together, iron carefully. Practise the technique on something small, like a cushion cover, but remember that patchwork can be made into simple garments and bedspreads.

Log cabin patchwork
This patchwork shape is also made from strips of fabric, sewn round and round a square, in a clockwise direction.

Choose two similar fabrics, one dark and one light.

Cut the fabric into strips along the grain of the fabric. Each strip should be at least 4 cm wide as anything less is very fiddly.

Cut about 5 cm of dark fabric and 5 cm light fabric. Pin and machine together, again using the machine foot as a guide for seam allowance. Keep adding strips along the top, down the right side, along the bottom and so on, trimming the end of the strip each time. Add two light and two dark alternately to give the illusion of a dark and light side to the finished shape.

Many blocks can be made and joined together to make a bedspread, or one block can be used for a cushion cover. Log cabin looks very beautiful when worked in corduroy using the channels as a guide when cutting the strips. It can also be successful in striped fabric, velvet or cotton. It has even been carried out successfully in a lightweight tweed. However, it is a good idea to start off by practising on cotton.

Apart from strips, squares, diamonds and triangles are also suitable for machine patchwork.

Construction of templates

A template should be as accurate as possible, drawn out on firm card with a hard sharp pencil.

The square

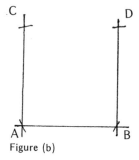

Figure (b)

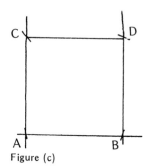

Figure (c)

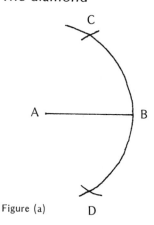

Figure (a)

Figure (a) draw a line and mark off the length of one side. AB

Figure (b) with a set square, draw a right angle at A and at B.

Mark off C and D so that AB = AC = CB.

Figure (c) join CD.

The diamond

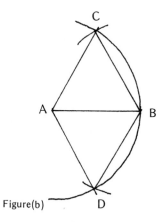

Figure (a)   D

Figure(b)   D

Decide the length of the side.

Figure (a) draw a semi-circle, radius = the length of the side of the diamond.

Join centre A to circumference B.

With compass point on B, draw an arc at C and D.

Figure (b) join AC, CB, AD, BC.

For a narrower (or fatter) diamond
Figure (a) Draw a line the width required AB.
Set compasses at the length of the side.
Put the compass point on A and draw an arc at C and D.
Put the compass point on B and draw arcs to cross at C and D.

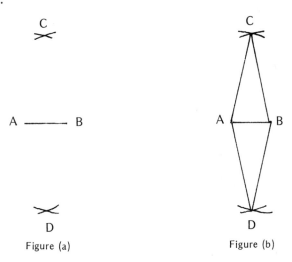

Figure (a)   Figure (b)

Figure (b) join AC, CB, BD, DA.
The triangle is half a square or half a diamond.

Seam allowance
Whatever the shape of your template it will need the addition of a seam allowance all the way round, before you cut it out.

When making machined patchwork it is easiest to make the seam allowance the distance between the machine needle and the outside right edge of the presser foot. The foot itself can then be used as a guide when machining. Measure this (it is usually about 7-9 mm) and add the measurement all the way round the shape. Cut out the template with a trimming knife, very accurately.

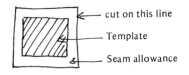

cut on this line

Template

Seam allowance

Squares

The easiest way of learning the technique of joining squares is to start by making a square from nine patches. Cut four light-coloured squares and five dark-coloured squares. Use a template and place the square onto the straight grain of the fabric. Draw round the template with sharpened tailor's chalk or a hard pencil (soft pencil smudges!) Pin and sew the patches into three strips. Pin and sew the strips together. Pin through the seams to ensure accuracy.

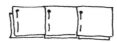

Squares can be used in many combinations to make patterns. These can be worked out on dressmaker's pattern guide paper. The squares can be composed of 5 x 5 patches, 6 x 6, 7 x 7 and so on. Remember that an odd number will give a centre square.

Large squares can be fitted in with four small squares, but work out the template sizes carefully and remember to leave a seam allowance for every patch.

Triangles

These can also be joined in strips, and can be used as border patterns as well as for areas of fabric.

Triangles can be mixed in with squares to make more interesting patterns. Look out for patchwork quilts in museums and sometimes in private houses.

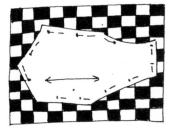

Diamonds

Diamond patches are joined in a diagonal strip and the strips are then machined together.

The placing of the pieces should be worked out carefully beforehand on paper, even-numbering the shapes so that they are in the right order. Even the simple patchwork which can be carried out on a sewing machine can be stunning if the right combination of colours and fabric patterns is chosen. Always be aware of how different fabrics tone or contrast with one another.

Strips of squares, diamonds and triangles are joined and made into an area of patterned fabric which can be used for dressmaking just like any other fabric. Iron carefully, place the pattern onto the fabric and cut out. If you are making a waistcoat, jacket, or anything with two matching sides, make sure both sides match by making two expanses of patchwork, one a mirror image of the other.

Textures

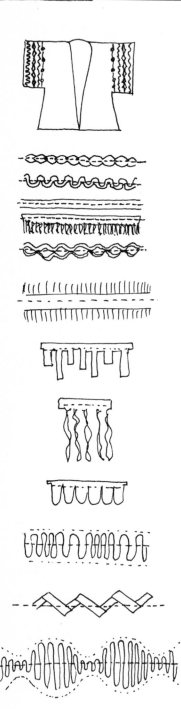

Fabric has a wide variety of different textures which make it versatile to use as a medium. For instance, satin feels cold and smooth, almost slimy and looks shiny. Wool tweed on the other hand feels hairy and warm and looks rough and nubby. There are several methods of creating interesting textures with a sewing machine, using various types of fabric and thread. Any of these might be incorporated into a hanging, or picture, or used to make clothes and accessories more interesting.

Couching

In hand embroidery, thick threads, metallic threads and threads which are impossible to sew, are couched onto the background with a thin thread and needle. In machine embroidery, the thick threads which will not go through the needle can be couched down with a row of machine stitches.

When using a straight stitch, the thread to be couched must be fairly thick so that it will easily take a line of machine stitches. Apart from thick threads like rug wool, ordinary knitting wool, metallic thread and weaving yarns can be plaited to make thicker threads.

Knitting cotton, crochet cotton and embroidery cotton can also be plaited or braided. Bindings, lace, ric-rac, ribbon and cords can all be couched with machine stitches. Even strips of non-fray knitted fabric like crimplene and jersey can be plaited and used as decoration. Strips of fabric can be cut on the cross, machined down the length, then turned inside out to make rouleaux, which can be plaited or braided.

Make use of fringe, both commercial and home-made, to add texture. Fringe can be cut in non-fray fabric, including leather, suede, PVC and felt.

When couching onto clothes, make sure the thread used will stand up to laundering.

For finer wools, or threads and for a different effect, zigzag the threads and sew across with straight stitch. Ribbon, cord or braid can also be used in this way.

Instead of pinning the thread you wish to couch onto the background, it is much easier to indicate the line of

7 Overlapping layers of padded finger shapes and wool loops

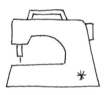

couching with a line of tailor's chalk, or poster paint and follow this with the machine and thread.

An all-over texture can be created by machining layer upon layer of looped thread, fringe, or rows of quilted shapes onto a background. Always start at the bottom and work up, overlapping layers. This is a useful texture for wall hangings and fancy dress. Use a strong background.

Fringe

It is possible to buy a tool which makes loops for use with a sewing machine. The tool is like a fork with two tines. The threads are wound round and round and the machine stitches between the two arms. As the machine goes forward, the fork is pulled forward so that the threads already attached by stitches fall off and more thread can be wound. The looped threads can be left as loops, or cut as tufts. Work from the bottom, so that the fringes overlap (see colour plate facing page 72)

A rather rough tool can be made by bending a length of wire (about 30 cm) into a U shape. Use wire about the thickness of a wire coat hanger.

Another attractive looped fabric can be made by making use of wide mesh scrim, or sacking. Using weaving yarn, pull the thread through from the back in loops, using a crochet hook. Start at the bottom of the fabric and work from left to right. When one row of loops has been pulled through, lock by machining across the top of the loops. This technique can be used for making rugs, or even a simple garment, apart from being very useful for making texture on a large wall hanging. The pulled threads do not have to be even. Some might be long and some short.

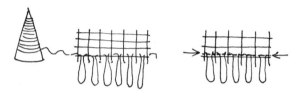

Weaving yarns were used in the sampler in the photograph, and rows of lustrous crochet cotton have been interspersed to add interest and a contrasting texture. However, any thread could be used, and it can be very rewarding to experiment with different knitting wools and cottons, metallic yarns, rug wools, carpet thrums, and even strips of fabric.

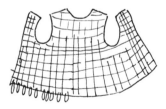

Block patterns

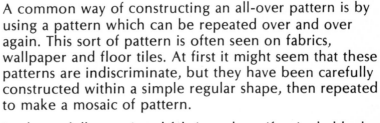

A common way of constructing an all-over pattern is by using a pattern which can be repeated over and over again. This sort of pattern is often seen on fabrics, wallpaper and floor tiles. At first it might seem that these patterns are indiscriminate, but they have been carefully constructed within a simple regular shape, then repeated to make a mosaic of pattern.

Look carefully at printed fabric and see if a single block of pattern has been repeated. Many patterns are printed in rectangular blocks which are arranged in squares, or like bricks.

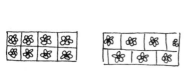

Triangles and hexagons can also be repeated in the same way, because rectangles, triangles and hexagons are regular shapes which will completely cover an area without leaving any spaces between the shapes.

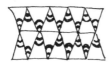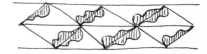

Quilting

Patterns and quilting go together admirably. Look at any quilted artifact, a bedcover, an anorak, even the inside of a jewel box, and see that it has been sewn with an all-over pattern. The pattern is even, to keep the wadding or stuffing spaced out for all-over warmth. Quilting has been used for hundreds of years, both on clothing and on bedding, to keep people warm before the advent of central heating. Nowadays, quilting and padding are used extensively in embroidery and on clothing, both for warmth and for added decoration and texture. There are several types of quilting which can be used, either together, or separately. They are all suitable for a straight stitch machine.

English quilting

In english quilting, a layer of padding, or wadding, is sandwiched between two layers of fabric, then sewn together with an all-over pattern.

The top layer
This is the fabric which will show. It can be any type of woven, smooth fabric, depending upon eventual use. It might be a printed cotton for a waistcoat, nylon for an anorak, or satin for an evening jacket. Non-stretch fabric is generally used for clothing and bedding, but it is interesting to experiment with stretchy knitted fabric, which will accommodate more wadding and thus create a very raised effect.

The middle layer
This is the padding, usually one, or several layers of cotton or terylene wadding. Never be tempted to use cotton wool. For a thin layer of wadding use flannel, or a similar piece of fabric. Foam-backed fabric can also be used. For a wall hanging, experiment with plastic foam. Make sure padding will launder if necessary.

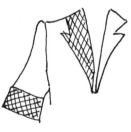

The bottom layer
This layer should match in with the top layer, if it is going to show, as it might on a waistcoat or bedcover. However, the fabric need not be so decorative, or expensive. Cotton, or polyester cotton, are suitable. If the backing is not likely to show, as on a wall hanging, or cushion cover, use cheesecloth, muslin or scrim.

Although quilting is often used on waistcoats, bags and bed coverings, it can also be used as a trim on collars, cuffs, pockets and hems. It is easy to buy a piece of fabric which has already been quilted, but it is possible to machine a more original design, or even add extra decoration to a commercial quilted fabric.

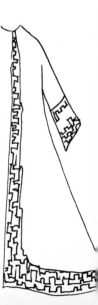

9 Quilting in straight lines on satin

Because the three layers of fabric need to be held together evenly, it is necessary to design an all-over pattern of stitches. These patterns can be made from the block patterns described on the previous page, using the triangle, rectangle and hexagon, all of which are made up of straight lines, easily managed by a straight stitch sewing machine and including a curved line pattern based on a repeating shape called an ogee.

The patterns can be constructed by crossing straight lines from left to right, then recrossing from top to bottom to make a grid.

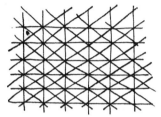 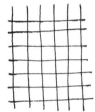 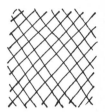

Alternatively, they can be taken as angled, or curved lines, from top to bottom, or from side to side, using a straight line as a guide.

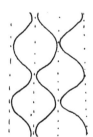 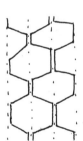 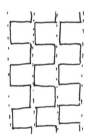 

It is also possible to decorate the grid patterns with continuous line patterns, thus combining the two.

These patterns can be worked out either on paper, or by doodling on the sewing machine, or a combination of both. The patterns do not have to be absolutely even. Irregular patterns can look interesting and original.

 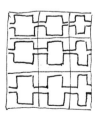 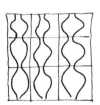  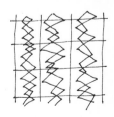

Preparation for quilting must be thorough. Iron both the top and bottom layer of fabric. If the fabric is to be quilted with a regular all-over pattern and then used to make into a garment, or part of a garment, it is a good idea to quilt the whole of the piece of fabric before cutting out.

Mark out the quilting design on the top layer.

If the design is based on a grid pattern or straight lines, both can be drawn with sharpened tailor's chalk and a ruler, or indicated with tacking stitches. The rest of the design can be drawn on the lines, or grid, with chalk, or can be worked freehand using the lines as a guide. (For other methods of transferring designs, see page 22.)

Lay the top fabric over the wadding and the bottom fabric. Start pinning and tacking, working from the centre out to the sides. Careless tacking, or pinning, at this stage, could result in puckers and unwanted gathers, so it is worth taking extra care over the preparation.

Make the first line of machine stitching the one which goes across the centre and work outwards.

Make use of fabrics with a regular pattern, stripes, checks and spots which can be quilted using the pattern as a guide. Irregular linear patterns based on curved and angled lines can be used in quilting, as well as motifs.

  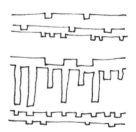 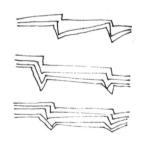

These have to be planned carefully, particularly on garments where both sides need to match.

The quilting should be planned onto the actual piece of pattern, marked out on the fabric, BUT NOT CUT OUT. However, the fabric with the pattern marked on can be cut away from the main piece of the fabric for ease of handling. The quilting is carried out in the same way, then the pattern pieces can be cut out from the background fabric and the garment made up. Although the pattern is irregular, the lines should be fairly evenly spaced without leaving any large gaps between lines, as the stitching keeps the wadding in place.

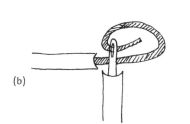

(a)

Italian quilting

This method makes use of two layers of fabric patterned with parallel lines of stitchery. The channel between the parallel lines is threaded with wool, quilting wool, cord, or string and makes a raised line (see figure a). It is possible to use a twin needle if the machine will take one, but by using two separate lines of stitches, the width can be extended to make a good fat line, or reduced to make a narrow one.

Italian quilting can be used to decorate dress, cushions, bags and wall hangings, but does not give the warmth of english quilting.

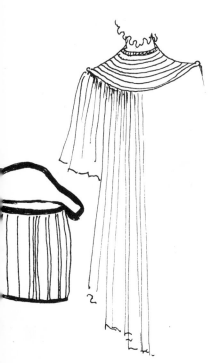

(b)

The top layer
This can be any smooth, firm fabric. It is interesting to use either translucent, or transparent fabrics, like chiffon, nylon and organdie and to use different coloured threads which will show through. Fabrics like crepe, satin, taffeta and silk also take italian quilting well.

Bottom layer
The backing can be polyester cotton, calico, muslin or fine scrim.

Quilting thread
Quilting wool can be obtained, but try various wools, piping cords and string to discover the different effects. Several threads can be used if necessary to give a good line. Remember that the thread should be washable and first tested for shrinkage, if the decoration is to be used on clothing. The quilting thread is threaded through the channel through the backing, using a large blunt needle. To turn corners take the needle out and push through at another angle (see figure b).

Leave a little ear of wool at each corner at the back to make a good angle. As machining makes a continuous line, it is a good idea to use a design which has no crossed lines. Rows of parallel lines in different widths look very effective and can be used as a block of decoration.

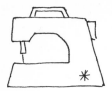

Trapunto quilting

This method also makes use of two layers of fabric. The effect is created by machining a motif, or a pattern, then padding out some of the enclosed areas with wadding, or kapok, from the back of the work, to make a raised area.

Top layer
For clothing, almost any smooth cloth will do, but experiment with stretch fabrics, knitted fabrics, stretch towelling.

Bottom layer
Muslin, tarletan or scrim, or some other fairly loosely woven fabric.

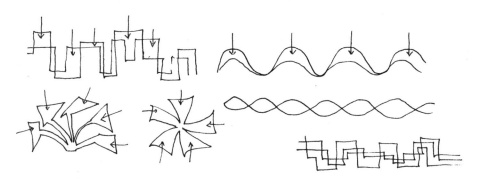

Choose a design which has an enclosed motif, or a linear design in which small islands are made where the lines cross. Tack the two layers together securely. Draw the design with sharp tailor's chalk or prick and pounce. Machine carefully. Turn. Cut slits in the backing and pad with kapok, wadding, or shredded tights, using a stiletto, or a large blunt needle, sew up slit by hand. Trapunto can be used with english quilting to add even more wadding to some areas. Be very careful, as the extra padding has to be pushed both through the backing and the layer of terylene wadding.

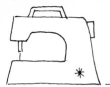

Shadow patterns

This is an easy and interesting way of using the square, diamond and triangular shapes normally used for patchwork. The shapes are cut from black, white, or coloured felt or some other non-fray fabric. The shapes are arranged on a base of firmly woven fabric. The shapes can then either be tacked, or lightly glued, onto the fabric base. The area is then covered with a piece of transparent or translucent fabric, such as organdie, chiffon or any similar fabric. Machine between the shapes, from top to bottom and from one side to another, machining between the small squares last.

Alternatively, two layers of translucent or transparent fabric can be used, with the shapes sandwiched between and held in place with stitches. Do not use glue if both sides are likely to be seen.

Experiment also with opaque fabrics like satin, fine leathers, PVC, perhaps using thicker felt in some places. Rather than always using shapes in a regular way, cut each into two, three or four pieces.

Arrange within the original shape. Machine across the main intersections then across the minor crossings. Use shapes that the machine can easily manage, like squares, triangles, diamonds and hexagons.

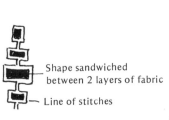

Shape sandwiched between 2 layers of fabric

Line of stitches

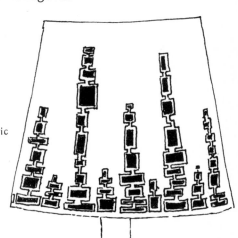

*10 A wall hanging
using english
quilting*

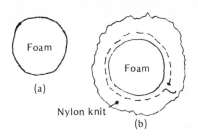

(a)

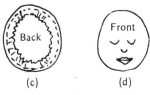

Foam

Foam

Nylon knit

(b)

Back

Front

(c)

(d)

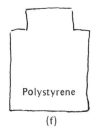

(e)

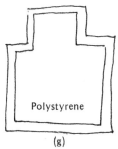

Polystyrene

(f)

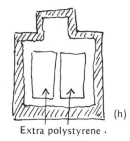

Polystyrene

(g)

(h)

Extra polystyrene .

The quilt
(Finished size; 24 cm x 23 cm). Any cotton fabric with a regular pattern can be used. Work out the quilting pattern on the fabric and mark with tailor's chalk, or tacking stitches. The flowers were painted with fabric paint. When the pattern has been planned, cut out the main fabric piece, leaving at least 5 cm spare fabric as a turning (29 x 28 cm).

Use two or three layers of wadding, cut to size (24 x 23 cm) and one layer of cotton, or muslin, for the bottom layer, cut slightly bigger than the wadding. Firmly pin and tack these layers together. Machine the pattern, starting in the centre and working out. When the quilting is finished, trim the bottom layer to the size of the wadding. Fold the edge of the top layer over both the bottom layer and the wadding, and then hem.

The pillow (20 x 10 cm)
Take a piece of the patterned fabric (25 x 15 cm) laid onto a piece of plain polyester cotton, three layers of wadding, (20 x 10 cm) and cotton or muslin backing. Plan and quilt a border pattern round the top and sides of the pillow. Cut away the patterned fabric in the middle to reveal the plain polyster cotton. Turn in the edge of the top fabric and hem.

The faces
Figure (a) Cut an oval of foam rubber.

Figure (b) Cut an oval of nylon knit (or tights) a little larger than the foam, and run gathering stitches round the edge.

Figure (c) Pull up and fit over the foam shape.

Figure (d) Indicate the features with hand stitches.

Figure (e) Sew the hair at the parting and arrange.

To make up.
Figure (f) Cut a polystyrene tile into the shape of the quilt and pillow, but 2 cm smaller.

Figure (g) Cover one side with fabric, bringing it about 4 cm round onto the other side.

Figure (h) Cut two pieces of extra polystyrene to raise the middle.

Sew the heads onto the pillow, sew the pillow onto the tile, using the fabric to hold the stitches.

Sew the quilt over the tile and over the bottom of the pillow.

Stick onto a larger mount.

49

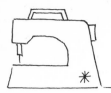

Pleating or tucking

This simple technique has been used on clothing for many years as a way of smoothing away excess fabric. It looks particularly beautiful on fine fabrics like polyester cotton, lawn and voile, but of course it can be used on any but the thickest of fabrics. Usually pleats are worked in regular rows, but these can look equally attractive when worked at random, some tucks near together and some far apart.

Tucks should be tried on a variety of fabrics, shiny and dull, to see the effect on each. Sew the tucks at random, using thread to match the fabric. It is easier to work from left to right, if you are right-handed. Try to make some tucks narrow, some wide, some close together, some wide apart, some widening and some narrowing. It is a good idea to practise on spare pieces of fabric, trying to get a balance between the wide and narrow pleats, and the wide and narrow spaces. Measure the fabric before starting the work and when it is finished, to see how much fabric your particular technique is likely to take, in case you wish to incorporate the pleating into a piece of work or an article of dress.

Pleated squares make unusual and successful patchwork. Blocks of pleats can be incorporated into a bodice, or used to

11 Irregular pleats on satin, decorated with zigzag stitch

50

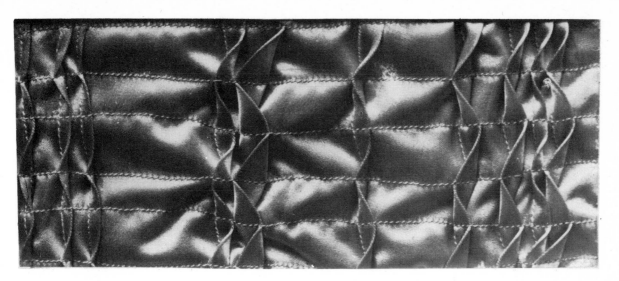

12 Satin reflects the light and gives a rich texture

trim a pocket. The pleated fabric can be used as an interesting basis for hand embroidery. If translucent fabric is used, or on any fabric, the channels can be threaded with wool, or cord.

These blocks of pleats, whether even or uneven, can be machined with lines of stitches at right angles to the pleats. The first machined line should push the pleats one way, the next line should push the other way, to give a texture similar to smocking. Try this out on fine fabrics, fabrics with spots, checks, stripes. If this texture is incorporated in dress, remember that it does not stretch like smocking, and should be treated as an ordinary piece of fabric.

Using textures to make a wall hanging

The textures made by couching, quilting and pleating, described over the last few pages, can be used in various ways to decorate dress and household accessories. They can also be used in wall hangings and embroideries, either as a background for hand embroidery, or as the main part of the embroidery. It is worth trying all of them, using a variety of fabrics to see the effects created. These textures and patterns can be grouped together in simple abstract designs, based on natural forms like flowing water and undulating landscapes, with the flowing lines which the machine can easily manage.

13 Various fabrics have been gathered, pleated and quilted, fringed, looped and then machined in layers onto the background

Choose a large variety of fabrics in tones of one colour. Select fabrics like hessian, frayed tweed, net, taffeta, stretch towelling, knitted nylon, cotton and so on, with textures to contrast and complement one another.

Arrange roughly in strips, just to get the idea of flowing lines and colours. Arrange fabrics with dark, ranging up to light, and light grading down to dark, or dark in the centre, working out to light. This is a chance to experiment. Try to decide which fabrics and colours look best together before starting to sew.

This is a very simple and effective method of designing, using textures and colours, but keeping within the capabilities of straight stitch sewing. When you have decided on the arrangement of colours, construct the textures on the sewing machine, before applying them to the background. Remember to use contrasting textures like pleated satin against looped wool, gathered net with quilted chiffon.

These flowing pictures can be planned more carefully, using a felt pen and drawing paper.

 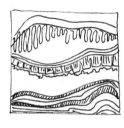 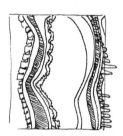

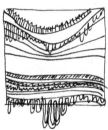 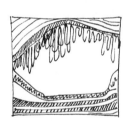 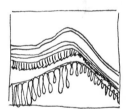

Draw a rectangle (7 x 10 cm) to contain the design.

Draw slightly curving lines from left to right, or from top to bottom. Look at the spaces between the lines, for these are also important. Some spaces might be uneven, some narrow, some wide.

At the same time, look out for designs in landscapes and seascapes, in flowing water and on the bark of trees, which might be carried out in machine textures. Do not be content with one or two attempts, but try several. The more you practise, the better you become. Experiment with colours and textures. In this way it is possible to construct an interesting, abstract wall hanging, which might fit into a particular place, or colour scheme.

The zigzag machine

Being able to make a zigzag line with a sewing machine widens the possibility of designs. It also gives a variation in width which can be used to enhance line patterns.

Look at the manufacturer's instructions for your machine.

There should be two controls for zigzag. The first will control the width of the zigzag stitch. This usually goes from a straight line to a width of 5 mm with several settings.

The second controls the density of the stitch, taking the stitch from a wide-spaced zigzag, to a closely-packed satin stitch.

Sometimes the top tension needs to be loosened slightly, when using the zigzag, so there is no possibility of the bottom thread pulling through and showing on the front of the work.

Make sure the machine is threaded properly, then using a spare piece of fabric, check that the machine will make an even zigzag, with correct tension.

Zigzag stitch will distort the fabric slightly and several rows of close satin stitch will pull considerably, so it is a good idea to strengthen the background fabric in some way. This can be done by backing with a piece of iron-on interfacing, or tacking a piece of cotton, or calico, to the back of the fabric. Alternatively, bond the calico, or cotton, to the background with bonding web. Fabric can also be held taut in an embroidery ring. If the background fabric is prepared in this way, the results will be much better.

Machine embroidery cotton is particularly suitable for zigzag where a lot of the thread shows on the surface.

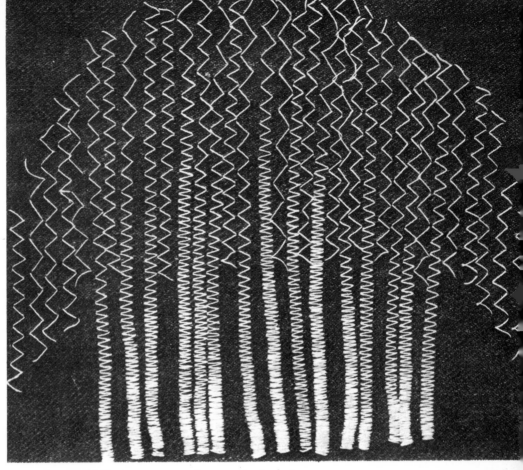

14 Tree patterns using graduated zigzag

Making patterns

First of all, practise with the stitch density control.

The machine makes a line varying from widely spaced zigzag, to satin stitch. The stitches are controlled by the knob, or lever, which can be turned, or pushed, as the machine is running, so that it will make an interesting line. The left hand controls the fabric, the right hand the control knob. Using a piece of prepared fabric, try out this technique, taking the stitch from satin stitch and grading out to wide zigzag. Counting from one to five as you twist the knob, or move the lever, helps to keep the pattern even.

It is always a good idea to try and produce some sort of pattern while practising.

Try parallel line patterns, lines crossing and lines exploding.

Keep the patterns for reference.

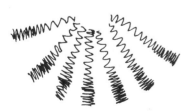

The continuous line-motifs and line-patterns described at the beginning of the book can be used with a zigzag stitch, and the variety of stitch widths can be used to make the pattern more interesting. Patterns based on rectangular shapes and angled lines look very good particularly if they are carried out accurately.

Try to make good sharp corners. To achieve this, zigzag, lift the foot and turn with the needle in the work, then zigzag across the last few stitches and so on.

Use an evenly woven fabric, and pull one of the threads to make a straight line to begin the pattern. Follow both the threads on the fabric and use the machine foot as a guide to keep the lines of stitches straight.

15 and 16 Continuous line patterns using narrow and wide zigzag

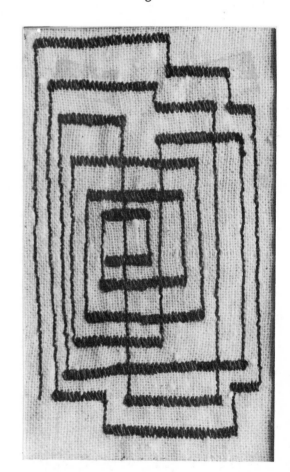

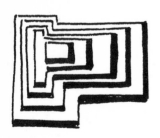

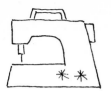

Fabric appliqué using a zigzag stitch

Fabric shapes can be cut out and attached to a background fabric with close zigzag stitch. This is a very good method of applying shapes to clothes as it is strong and will stand up to laundering. Choose a design which makes use of straight lines and curves which are not too acute for the machine to manage.

When applying fabric shapes to garments, it is a good idea to use similar fabrics so that there is no problem when laundering or cleaning.

Cut out the fabric pieces so that the grain of the applied shape and the grain of the background run the same way. If this is impossible, line the fabric shape with iron-on interfacing, applied before cutting out. Do not use very small pieces, as these are difficult to handle. Any detail can be indicated with straight stitch, or satin stitch lines.

Place on the background. Pin and tack securely, or bond onto the background. Go round the shape with an open zigzag to attach the shape, then go round again with a close zigzag, or satin stitch.

Leather and suede patchwork
Leather and suede patchwork shapes can be joined with a zigzag stitch to make really beautiful patchwork cushions or even bedspreads. Cut the leather pieces absolutely accurately with a trimming knife, leaving no seam allowance.

Hold the pieces together with sticky tape. These should abut, but not overlap. Zigzag with a medium open stitch, as satin stitch can weaken the leather so that it pulls away. Fine leather and suede will sew with an ordinary machine needle, but it is also possible to buy a special sewing machine needle for leather.

Practice first on small pieces of leather.

17 A design made up entirely of straight lines is easy to work on any machine

Reverse appliqué with zigzag stitch

When using a straight stitch, reverse appliqué must be carried out on non-fray fabrics, but with close zigzag it is possible to use any sort of fabric, as the stitches stop the material from fraying out. Although cotton is the easiest fabric to use, some very exciting reverse appliqué can be done, using layers of net, organdie, chiffon, satin, brocades and silks, as well as velvet, fine wool, rayon, and so on. Where reverse appliqué is to be used on clothes, the fabrics should all be washable.

Choose a simple design which can be maneuvred easily on a machine. The design should include enclosed shapes which are easy to cut out. Avoid very narrow shapes or very acute angles.

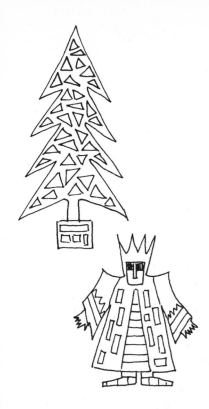

Making a reverse appliqué motif with four layers of fabric (36 mm x 27 mm)

Choose four pieces of cotton or cotton polyester, about 36 mm x 27 mm. The four fabrics should look well together, but at the same time they should contrast with the adjacent layer, both in colour and pattern, so that they can easily be seen.

For the motif in the photograph four layers were chosen.

Top layer: horizontal stripes, ranging from dark to light.
Second layer: dark background, bright, small-print flowers.
Third layer; vertical, narrow, pale stripes.
Bottom layer; plain, dark, cotton.

1   Cut four pieces of fabric about 36 mm x 27 mm Cut on the straight grain, so that the grain of the fabrics all run the same way. Pin and tack securely in the right order, otherwise the fabrics will slip when they are machined. Tack both round the edge and across the middle.

2   Trace the design and transfer onto the top layer of fabric (see page 22). Choose a neutral thread which can be used throughout the work.
Test the tension at the edge of the fabric sandwich, where it will not show, and tie off the threads at the back, at the end of each step.

3   Using 2 mm, satin stitch, machine round each star shape. Cut out the top layer of fabric inside the star shapes using sharp, pointed scissors. Cut carefully, in order not to cut through the stitches. (If you have the misfortune to cut through the second layer by mistake, slip a piece of bonding fabric behind the cut and iron.)

4   Machine round the outside edge of the stem and branches. It will be necessary to stop at the star and start again at the other side. Cut away the top and second layer within the shape, to reveal the third layer.

5   Machine round the inside shape of the stem and branches. Cut away the third layer within the shape to show the bottom layer.

6   Run your finger nail down the edge of the cut fabric and stitches and cut away the whiskers.

7   Iron.

Experiment with reverse appliqué, both with colour and pattern and with various fabrics.

59

Cut work with zigzag stitch

Cut work is carried out on a single layer of fabric. Like reverse appliqué the design used should have plenty of enclosed spaces. After machining round the design in satin stitch, these enclosed shapes are carefully cut out.

The technique looks really pretty on fine, but strong, woven fabrics like organdie, cotton polyester, voile and lawn. It can be worked as a border pattern, or a motif. Try both narrow and wide satin stitch. The thread can either match, or contrast with the fabric used, but a matching thread gives a beautiful effect.

Try the technique on both light and dark coloured fabric as each has a completely different look.

18 Cut work on organdie

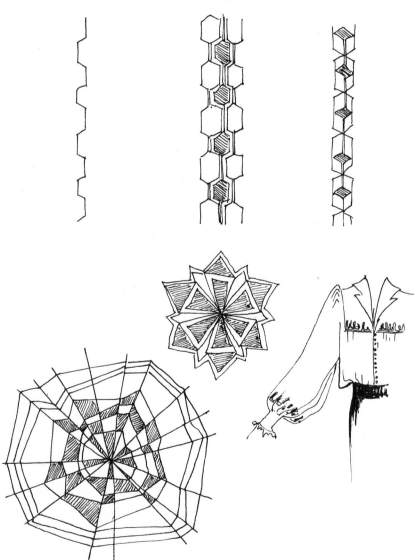

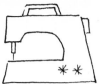

Couching with zigzag stitch

Any thread, including fringe, cord, or braid, can be couched to a background with zigzag stitch.

The width and density of the zigzag can alter the appearance of the couched thread. Think of the stitch as an added decoration to the couching, as well as a way of attaching it.

Try both narrow and wide zigzag stitches, not only down the middle of the thread, but perhaps down the side instead. The thread might tone in, or contrast with the couched thread.

Couching with satin stitch produces a raised, cordlike line, which is very attractive. Use thin string, piping cord, or firm wool, as a base thread. It is easier to draw the design straight onto the background with tailor's chalk, then follow the lines with the thread and machine. First attach the thread with zigzag stitch, then go over it again with close satin stitch.

To make a good angle, stop with the needle in the fabric on the inside of the angle. Pull the couched thread round the needle.

Maze-like patterns are both decorative and interesting. They can be planned on paper. Draw a square, circle, or similar regular shape. Starting at one edge, take a line round the shape in straight and angled lines, filling the shape completely with a continuous line pattern. Couching can be incorporated in wall hangings, or used as dress decoration.

19 A continuous line pattern using zigzag over string

Graduation in width of zigzag stitch
Satin stitches worked on a sewing machine can be graduated from wide to narrow and back again, by controlling the fabric with the left hand, and the width setting with the right hand. There is no doubt that this is very taxing and difficult, needing a lot of practice and very good control of the machine.

Start by practising straight lines, tapering and widening. Taper the lines over several mm, then contrast by tapering over just a few mm. The line should be smooth. It can help to count as you turn the dial, or push the lever.

Having mastered straight lines, try curved, tapered lines, as curved as the machine will allow. You can get a little more curve by loosening the pressure on the foot, if that is possible on your machine.

As you machine, try to watch the fabric and the pattern you are making, and turn the dial without looking.

The machine will make flowing lines and angled lines and it is even possible to get away with rounded shapes by altering the direction of the stitches. If you can persevere with this technique, it opens up the possibility of pictures and patterns worked entirely in satin stitch, using a graduated line which is much more delicate and sensitive than a straightforward zigzag.

Practise for a few minutes every day, rather than for several hours at a time.

This is a good opportunity to use some of the graduated machine-cottons which are available. Fabric paint can also be used, to add patches of colour. With the top tension loosened slightly, so that the bottom thread is not likely to show, a neutral colour can be used in the bobbin, then it is only necessary to change the top colour.

This technique can be used with applied fabric shapes and is suitable for both dresses and embroidery. The background fabric for wall hangings should be backed with interfacing or bonded to a piece of cotton, or muslin, to keep it firm. For a dress, keep the fabric taut in an embroidery ring.

20 This scene is worked in tapering zigzag, in straight and slightly curving lines

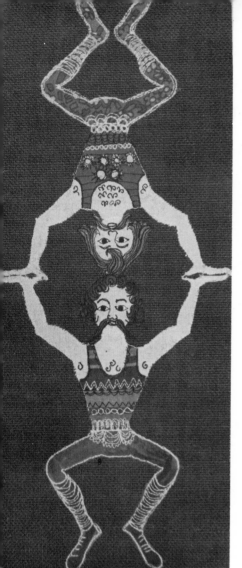

21 Acrobats. Free machine embroidery on applied fabric shapes

Free embroidery

Free embroidery can be done on any foot controlled sewing machine, ie treadle or electric. Hand operated machines are impossible, as the fabric has to be held in both hands.

The feed dog pulls the fabric through the machine so that it moves forward (see page 10). If the feed dog is removed, however, the fabric stays in one place and the machine sews on the spot. If the fabric is then moved by the operator, it can be moved in any direction free of the feed dog. That is why it is called free embroidery. It is possible to sew forwards, backwards and sideways with ease. This means that absolutely any design or pattern can be worked on a sewing machine.

Preparation of the machine
Look at the manufacturer's instructions to find out how to darn. This usually entails using a special darning foot and the removal of the feed dog.

If you have no instructions, you will find that the feed dog can be removed, or covered, in one of the following ways.

1 By pressing a knob or lever, you will find that the feed dog slides down into the machine.

2 The metal plate surrounding the feed dog is called a throat plate. It is sometimes possible to buy a throat plate specially made for darning and embroidery, which is raised so that the feed dog cannot come in contact with the fabric.

3 On older machines, treadle or electric conversions, the feed dog can be unscrewed and removed. If you do this, make sure you are able to replace it again afterwards.

Most machines have a darning foot. If not, free embroidery can be done by removing the foot altogether, but be careful of your fingers.

You may find that it is possible to buy a darning foot for an old machine. Many sewing machine specialists keep accessories for very old, as well as new machines.

Preparation of the background fabric for free embroidery
It is essential that the background fabric should be taut. If

the material is not held in some way, the machining puckers it considerably. (This actually gives rather a pleasant texture which might be put to use elsewhere). There are several ways of holding the material taut.

1   An embroidery ring

Special steel embroidery rings are sold by machine specialists. These can be anything between 5 cm and 12 cm in diameter, and are very efficient. An ordinary wooden embroidery ring is also satisfactory. Use a small diameter to start with. The inner ring should be bound with tape. This binding holds the fabric more securely as well as preventing the wood from snagging the fabric. Plastic rings are unsatisfactory as the fabric is apt to spring out. Embroidery rings are used for free embroidery on fine fabrics and for dress embroidery.

2   Paper-backed fabrics

Paper-backed hessian is sold as wallpaper and makes excellent background material for machine embroidery. The colours and texture are good, and the backing keeps the fabric taut enough not to distort. It is expensive, however, and any fabric can be bonded onto paper quite easily using PVA glue. Choose a strong woven fabric, like hessian, soft furnishing fabrics, linen type dress fabrics etc. Cover lining paper with a thin, even layer of PVA glue. Lay the fabric over the glued paper and smooth out any wrinkles and bulges, then iron the fabric onto the paper. Turn, and iron on the paper. Have the iron at the hottest possible setting without burning the fabric, or the paper. The heat causes the glue to bond the fabric and the paper together. This sort of background is very good for an appliqué picture with a lot of added fabric and thread. Because the backing is wallpaper, the finished hanging can be pasted with wallpaper paste and hung like a piece of wallpaper on hardboard. Thus the background is kept

22 Fishing in the channel. Free machine embroidery on applied fabric shapes

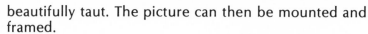

beautifully taut. The picture can then be mounted and framed.

3 Iron-on interfacing
This is only suitable for small pieces of work.

4 Vanishing muslin
This material is tacked onto the back of the fabric, then when the work is finished, it is ironed with a hot iron and the vanishing muslin disintegrates. It is good for dress, or wall hangings, or pictures.

5 Fabric can be dipped in cellulose paste (wallpaper paste) spread out, or pushed into three dimensional shapes and dried (see page 105).

The technique

Free embroidery is a skill which anyone can learn with enough practice. Some people can pick up the knack immediately, while others can take weeks. On average it takes ten hours of practice to make controlled patterns without continually breaking the thread and losing your temper. Free embroidery is well worth mastering.

Start by practising on some paper-backed fabric. You will need a large needle.

1 Place the fabric under the needle and lower the foot. Always make sure that the foot is down. With a darning foot, or no foot at all, it is not easy to tell whether the presser foot is up or down.

2 Bring the bottom thread up to the top by turning the flywheel, and hold both threads to the back of the fabric. Hold these threads until you have sewn a few stitches, then cut off. There is no need to finish them off at the back.

3 Start with the needle almost touching the fabric and begin to sew. As the feed dog is not there to move the fabric, you have to do this yourself. Hold the fabric flat with both hands, and gently push backwards and forwards, round and round. Keep the fabric flat on the base of the machine and mind your fingers.

Try to relax and make both the driving of the machine and the movement of the fabric as smooth as possible. Practise for about 15 minutes at a time, backwards and forwards, round and round until you are reasonably proficient.

23 Butterfly shape applied to cotton jersey tee-shirt with free machine embroidery

In the first part of this book, it was shown that border patterns and motifs could be formed from straight, angled and slightly curved lines. This is still true, but without the control of the feed dog, the machine is also capable of making very tight curves, so that any pattern can be attempted. It is still easier to use a continuous line pattern to avoid continually having to stop, finish off and start again.

Using a prepared background, try out patterns based on tight curves and spirals. Build up lines of patterns in the same way as before, starting with an uncomplicated curvy line which can then be decorated.

It is possible to build up patterns, both regular and irregular, which can be used as border patterns and motifs on dress and home furnishings. Remember to make use of different fabrics. These patterns can be used to enhance a printed motif and also to attach appliqué shapes to a background in a more interesting way than a straight line.

Machine-embroidered patterns are never as precise as automatic patterns. In fact their charm lies in the fact that they often turn out slightly irregular. Practise so that it becomes easy to sew a pattern. Pulling out is difficult and tedious, so try to incorporate small mistakes. The pattern can first be chalked on the fabric, but it is more interesting and creative to doodle on a background, just to see what sort of pattern arises, basing the doodles on the sort of writing patterns and pothooks used when learning to write.

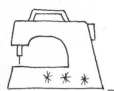

Machine embroidery on paper-backed fabric — making a butterfly

Butterflies, moths and insects make very pretty designs and motifs. This butterfly has been worked on paper-backed hessian to make a picture (23 x 23 cm), but a similar shape could also be applied to clothing, using a 26 cm, diameter embroidery ring (see pages 65 and 82). For clothes and soft furnishing, make sure all fabrics will launder.

A butterfly provides a good excuse to use scraps of exotic fabric like brocade, silk, satin, taffeta. See collections of butterflies and moths in museums and encyclopedias for inspiration in colour and shapes.

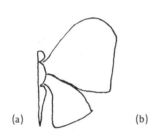
(a)
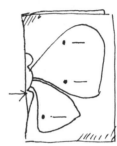
(b)

(c)

Instructions

Figure (a) Draw one half of a butterfly shape on a piece of paper. (See diagram on page 115.)

Do not forget the head and body.

Figure (b) Fold a piece of iron-on interfacing in half. Put the head and body at the fold and pin the shape to the interfacing. Cut out.

Figure (c) Open out the butterly shape.

Choose a piece of fabric and iron the interfacing shape to the back. Cut out the shape. Prepare a piece of paper-backed fabric 23 cm x 23 cm. Pin, tack or stick the shape onto the background fabric. Do not use glue for clothing.

With matching thread, attach the shape all round the edge, starting at the head and working out to the right side, then the left. Always work out from the centre to keep the shape flat. Sew the first line of stitches a couple of mm from the edge.

Cut the spots for the wings from contrasting fabric. Cut two spots at a time on folded fabric. Place the spots in position to see how they look.

The spots and shapes can be lightly glued, or pinned into place and machined.

Use contrasting thread, or black and try to make the lines of stitching form patterns on the wings. Sew an interesting pattern on the head and body, and remember to stitch antennae and eyes.

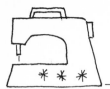

Simple shapes for pictures

Make use of simple shapes to build a picture. Fabric shapes can be cut out, applied and decorated with pattern to add interest. Choose a firm background, like a paper-backed fabric, for appliqué. This fabric picture is based on a line of rectangles and makes use of small printed fabrics, cut-out flowers and spot shapes which have been further decorated. Start and finish as little as possible, trying to make use of continuous line patterns.

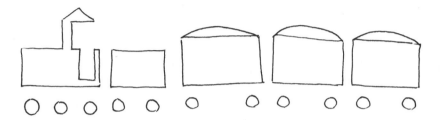

Do not use very small pieces of fabric, which will disintegrate under the needle. Sew any details with the machine.

Think of objects with simple shapes which might be treated in a decorative way, like boats, vintage cars, fish and birds.

Looking for ideas for pictures

Many people feel that they would like to embroider a picture, not an abstract pattern, or an ethnic textured hanging, but an original, realistic picture. The difficulty arises when it comes to choosing a subject, particularly for a beginner and sometimes for quite experienced embroiderers. It takes practice to pick out an idea from an environment which is made up of endless designs, both man-made and natural. Do you want to represent a townscape, a street of houses, a single building, or the pattern of mildew and moss on a single brick? Do you want a picture of a forest, a glade of trees, a young sapling, a branch of blossom, or the pattern of veins on a leaf? It is really a matter of learning to look, to choose, to pick out and isolate an interesting design from all the others surrounding it.

Try this experiment: Look out of the window. You are confronted with a jumble of colours, shapes and patterns. Even a brick wall has colour and texture. Try to pick out six objects. By doing this, you have isolated six potential designs. These particular designs may not appeal to you, but by continually isolating ideas in this way, you are beginning to train yourself to look.

Always keep watch: when you are waiting at the
supermarket checkout; at the bus stop; sitting in a traffic
jam; at the doctor's surgery; walking the dog; meeting the
children; be on the alert for ideas. In every situation,
make yourself isolate two or three ideas, until you get
into the habit of doing this automatically.
Collect ideas because you yourself like them, and not
because they are considered picturesque by other people.
Industrial scenery, motorways and factories can be just as
visually exciting as a field of buttercups, or a sunset over
the sea. It really depends on what appeals to you
personally.

Keeping a record
Try to write down ideas as they occur, even if it means
jotting them roughly on a scrap of paper. It is a good idea
to keep a sketch book, even if you feel you cannot draw
very well. Many people cannot draw in a very expert way,
but still successfully manage to get a rough idea of what
they want to do on paper. Try to accept the fact that your
plans will not necessarily look like the professional
printed design you might buy in a shop, but which will
also have been bought and worked by countless other
people. Your designs will have the tremendous advantage
of being unique, which is very important, particularly in
an age of mass-production. You will also find that you will
become more confident and improve as you find more
ideas and do more designing.

Opposite

Swiss mountain   *The grass was*
made from fringe (see pages
38-39) and the flowers were
machined with a loosened
bobbin, cut out and applied

72

When you come across an idea you like, try to sketch it in your book, using rough rectangular shapes, just to show the position of the objects in the picture. Use words to describe colour, texture, patterns. You can make use of photographs to help with shapes and details. This is a page from a sketchbook showing an idea taken from a television programme. (*See also* page 108.)

Man black beret
Coat + string belt
Wellingtons
All white
Sheep horns
Black faces + legs
Oblong bodies
Put man further left
Dog forward a bit
Trees blowing sideways
V.cold. windy. (W. from l—r)
Bl. & white dog?
Leaning in wind.

Opposite

Sledging *Free machine embroidery on fabric appliqué. Effective buildings can be made from rectangles of fabric. Small patterned fabric is suitable for clothing*

Opposite

Crows on the motorway *Free machine embroidery on fabric appliqué. The background is paper-backed hessian*

In these circumstances, it is imperative to get down any information as quickly as possible, and fill in details later, either from memory, or with the help of photographs. A picture does not often present itself like this, and most designs have to be worked out painstakingly, moving the shapes round and round until they make a satisfactory composition.

Without copying their work, try to analyse the way in which other people turn their ideas into paintings, sculpture, embroideries, prints and tapestries.

Facing this page is an example of how one idea was turned into a fabric picture. Travelling by motorway, most people have noticed the carrion crows which flutter around the hard shoulder, looking for tit-bits, in spite of the heavy lorries continually thundering past only inches away.

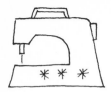

These birds seem to have come to terms with modern life and have even turned it to their advantage.

When planning a picture, two aspects are important, and should be carefully considered before beginning to sew. The first is the composition, which is the way in which everything is set out. The second is the detail of the shapes, the colours and the fabrics.

Composition
Before anything else, decide what is important and cannot be left out of the picture. Which objects must be included to get across the idea. In this particular design, the crows, the motorway and the lorries were basic and had to be there.

Next decide how the important objects should be arranged to best effect and from what angle they should be seen. A lorry can be viewed from any angle, front, back, side, top, underside. However, machined appliqué is flat and does not take kindly to perspective, so it seemed very much easier and more practical to depict the vehicles from the side. That meant that the motorway itself would run across the picture, with the birds in the foreground.

The next point to consider is the size of the objects in the picture. Is there going to be one very large bird and only the wheels of a lorry; or a group of fairly large birds and several vehicles in the background; or a flock of birds and streams of vehicles? You have to decide which will have

26 and 27 Details of colour plate facing page 73

most impact, which will best communicate your idea to the person who is looking at the picture. Again, it is a matter of choice, which must be made before arranging the objects in their final position.

Arrangement
The objects should be arranged so that they fill the picture comfortably, without being too crowded or too sparse. To avoid the perspective of one row of lorries behind the other, and also to fill the rectangle more satisfactorily, the lorries and cars were arranged on a split-level motorway. The composition can be arranged within a rectangle, using simple cut-out paper shapes to represent the objects in the picture. Shuffle the shapes about to get the very best possible composition. Take plenty of time, then, when you are satisfied, stick the shapes down.

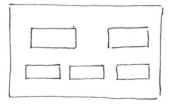 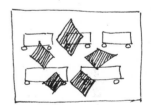

It is easy to describe this process which starts with a vague idea and finishes with a rough plan of a picture, but in fact it can take anything from a few minutes to several years. The plan might work out easily and immediately, or it might take a lot of thought over months before the final design comes into being.

Always write down, or draw ideas, in case you forget something which might have been useful. The final picture will be much more satisfactory if you start off with a clear idea of what you want to do, and how you want to set it out. It is worth taking time.

Details
When a design is running through your head it is a good idea to collect details at the same time. One day, the idea will gell, and then time will have been saved by collecting together as much information as possible about the objects in the picture. In this particular design, it was necessary to look at vehicles. The basic body shape of most vehicles is rectangular. Usually, articulated lorries are variations on a cab with a trailer. The load on the trailer is what makes one lorry look different from another. It is possible to find lorries and cars parked both in car parks and at the side of the road, either to draw, or to take photographs. Birds are more difficult, but it is a good idea to watch not just crows but all birds, to see how they behave, move, take off, fly and land. Again, photographs are a great help, as well as trying to draw or cut out, even roughly, some general outline.

At the same time look out for suitable fabrics. The right colour, the right sheen, the right texture can help tremendously to get across an idea. Let the material help you. The fabric should never get between you and what you want to create. If it does, throw it away and find something else. When dealing with rectangular shapes, make use of the fact that many fabrics are woven on a rectangular basis with weft and warp.

When the idea finally clicks into place, you will have plenty of detailed information to help you carry it out in fabric and thread.

The final plan
Now is the time to work out a detailed scale plan. Use a piece of paper the same size as the finished picture will be. From the sketches and photographs work out the main shapes in the right proportions. Pin the shapes onto the background. Pin the plan onto the wall and stand several feet away from it, to see if the shapes and the spaces between the shapes are well balanced. If you do not like the placing, unpin the shapes and rearrange them until you do. If the plan is satisfactory, stick the shapes down. There is no need to fill in details. This plan should not be destroyed.

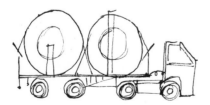 

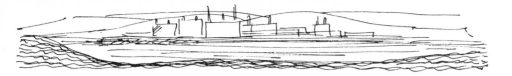

The background

An appliqué picture might be quite large, so a paper-backed fabric is most suitable as it is heavy enough to take layers of fabric and machine stitches without puckering (See page 65).

The background should contrast with the foreground, complement it, throw it into sharp relief. Usually a background is lighter in tone, so that the darker foreground shows up. The background might just be the paper-backed fabric used by itself, or with two or three strips of fabric added for interest. On the other hand it might be built up of layers and strips of fabric, some superimposed, some adjacent, decorated with machine stitch patterns. All the fabrics for the picture should be chosen as the plan is taking shape. Pin these fabrics to a wallboard and look at them from a distance. Some colours are dominant and seem to leap forward. They are not always suitable for a background.

Very textured fabric like tweed, corduroy, fringes and so on, are best used in the foreground. Smooth, pale fabrics make good backgrounds; satins, taffetas, dupion, net, chiffons and nylon can be superimposed to give lovely sky and water effects. Buildings, trees, hills can be cut out in pale fabrics and attached with light-coloured cotton. Try not to use very small pieces of fabric. Of course, these directions are only very general, and it is always worthwhile experimenting with your own ideas.

It is important to plan and cut out the whole of the background before finally sewing. Also have to hand the fabric you intend to use in the foreground, just to make sure you know how it is going to look.

28 Cords, fringes and knots can be applied to a picture to give texture

Indicate the position of the main pieces on the background with tailor's chalk. Put all the fabric pieces onto the masterplan to keep them in order. They can then be taken from the plan to the background, one by one.

The pieces can then be pinned and sewn, tacked and sewn, or sewn freehand, using the chalk marks as a guide. There is no need to turn in the edges. Only use fabric glue very sparingly as the machine is apt to push the fabric against the glue and make puckers.

Start sewing from the centre out to the edge, then back to the centre and out to the other edge. Pull the fabric into place as you sew. Attach each piece of fabric with lines of stitches, either straight or in patterns, every 2-5 cm to make the fabric lie flat. If the lines of stitching are too far apart, the fabric will twist. When the background fabric is attached, decorate with more stitches if necessary.

To make a sharper edge, on a horizon, on water and so on, sew across the strip of fabric, then fold it over and sew down.

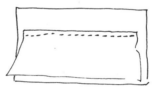 

Use a large, sharp, machine needle when sewing on paper-backed fabric. Always try to use simple, manageable shapes, using the stitch patterns for details.

The background chosen for the motorway picture was paper-backed hessian. Part of this was left as sky,

29 The background of the colour plate facing page 73 is composed almost entirely of rectangles of fabric attached with straight machine stitch, decorated with free machine embroidery

30 Chiffons, georgettes and translucent fabrics can be used to cover satin or dupion to create a luminous effect

patterned with lines of stitches to indicate clouds. The carriageways, grass and hard shoulder were long strips of contrasting fabric, attached with lines of machine stitches, some close together and some wide apart.

The size and general shape of everything should have been worked out on the masterplan. Now this information has to be translated into fabric and stitches.

Appliqué is not suitable for very narrow strips of fabric or intricate shapes and these should be carried out in machine stitch patterns. The general outline shape is the most important. Very simple shapes can be cut from fabric and applied, then the details are drawn on afterwards with machine stitches. Freehand cutting is a useful skill. It is possible to construct winter trees with strips of fabric, not too thin, for the twigs can be added with stitches. Flowers can be worked from a circle of fabric, houses and vehicles from rectangles.

More complicated shapes of birds and animals can be blown up from a photograph or sketch, but the shape should be simplified as much as possible. Some people find it easier to draw a shape within a rectangle, so that the edges of the objects touch the sides. It is most helpful to know how an object is made, how it grows, or how it works. Cut out the shapes and arrange on the background. Pin, tack, or lightly glue, and machine from the middle, working out where possible. Make all the details with machined patterns. The machine will make any complicated pattern you like.

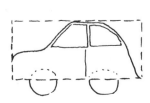

People in pictures

Do not be afraid to include people in pictures. There are few places so lonely that a couple of people cannot be seen somewhere. It might seem difficult to represent a human body. People come in different shapes and sizes; thin and fat, tall and small, bent and straight, and they are always moving about. But the general proportions of the body are about the same in all people.

Everyone has a model in himself and can look in a mirror to see how each joint bends and how the body is balanced. Look at yourself and try to imagine that you can see your skeleton shape. The head takes up about a seventh of the body height, although a child's head is bigger in proportion. The shoulders act like a coat hanger and from them the arms and hands hang down to the top of the thighs. The elbow tuck into the waist. The hands are quite big. Outstretched, they cover the face from chin to forehead. The hip line is about halfway down the body. All these proportions are general, but useful if you are to include figures in a scene. Find out which way you can bend. Look at yourself standing and sitting. How do you balance? Look at the way people are represented in paintings, sculptures, photographs and drawings. Watch people moving about, walking, running, playing games, dancing. Watch them sitting, talking, standing, leaning.

Watching people makes it possible to construct stickmen, which can be used in pictures. These can be drawn, or made from strips of paper cut in the right proportions. Practise making groups of stickmen who are engaged in some activity like playing football, sitting, or standing and talking, skating, and so on. Try to make them look interesting by putting them in different positions. People move their hands and heads when they talk. Even when they are standing still, they move their legs and feet and their arms and hands. It is rare to see a person standing stiffly to attention.

Make the stickmen at least 7-10 cm, if you want to dress them in fabric clothes. Smaller people should be completely machined, clothes and all. Cut out the shapes of the clothes, sleeves and body separately, then skirt or trousers. Use very small prints, checks, stripes and plain cottons. It is easier to machine the hands in flesh-coloured thread, unless the figure is large, and the hand shapes can be cut out of fabric and applied. Feet can also be applied and should not be too small. The face can be a simple oval, with features machined, or sewn by hand.

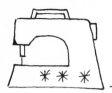

Machine embroidery with a ring

An embroidery ring can be used for machine embroidery to keep the fabric taut, and this is the most suitable way of decorating dress and soft furnishings.

It is possible to embroider on any fabric which will comfortably go into an embroidery ring. Use one layer, or even two or three layers of fabric.

Practise with a small ring (see page 65) and a piece of firmly woven fabric like cotton or calico. Felt is a very good fabric for practice, as it is easy to manage.

Remove the feed dog and attach an embroidery foot, or darning foot, or remove the foot altogether. Tension should be normal.

Put the ring under the machine as if it were a saucer. Bring the bottom thread to the surface and hold both threads until two or three stitches have been worked. Drive the machine smoothly.

Work with the ring resting on the base of the machine, only lifting it enough to move it around, and make patterns with the machine. With this method, only a small area can be worked within the ring. However, it is easy to move the ring from place to place, making sure the fabric is always taut. Embroidery on dress must be carried out before the pieces are cut out. Mark the position of the pieces with chalk. Heavy machining can distort the fabric slightly, so the pattern piece might need adjustment.

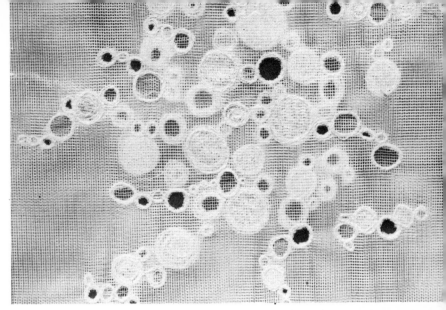

32 *Several layers of net machined in a pattern based on circles. Some circles can then be cut away*

Circles and spirals in design

With free embroidery, the machine can make any curved shape, so now it is possible to use the circle as a basis for design. Practise doodling with circles, arranged in lines and groups, both big and small, on a piece of fabric held in a ring.

Plan similar designs by cutting out circle shapes from paper. Cut various sizes and arrange them in interesting groups. Try an exploding pattern, with the mass of circles in the centre, petering out on all sides. Try a group of circles with some shapes superimposed on top of one another. These sorts of designs look very attractive on dress. The machine line is still continuous, so it is far easier to join the circles than to keep stopping, finishing off and starting again. This means using a spiral, which will join one circle with the next. Try to make flowing lines.

Many fabrics can be used, or two or three layers of fabric for reverse appliqué.

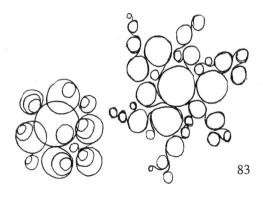

83

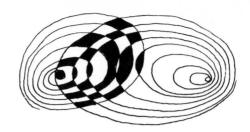
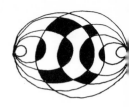

Overlapping spiral patterns can be worked on two layers of contrasting fabric, perhaps one black and one white. Parts of the top layer can then be cut away to reveal the layer beneath.

Circles can be arranged on curving lines to give another useful design. To plan, cut out a lot of paper circles, more than you will need, so that you will have plenty of choice. Draw a curved line, perhaps a letter S, and arrange the circles almost touching and overlapping the curved line. It is a good idea to group several of the larger circles together as a focal point on the line, and allow the rest to taper off gradually. Try this using other curved letters C J O U.

If a fabric will go into a ring, and stay taut, it can be embroidered, so try out different fabrics, like organdie, satin, cotton, etc.

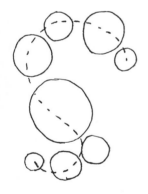

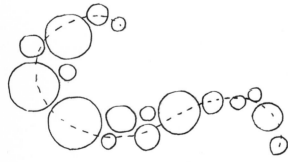

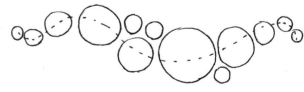

A circle can be used as a shape within which to make a flower. Many flowers are more or less circular, although made up from radiating petals of various shapes. This is useful, as the design can be worked out in circles which can then be turned into flowers. Freehand circles always look more natural in any design. Make a note of petal shapes which might be used, and make a collection of flowers which would fit into a circular motif.

The flowers can be worked in several ways.

A circle of coloured fabric can be applied as a colour base and the details of petals can be machined in a continuous line pattern. The circular shape can be indicated in tailor's chalk and then the details can be machined as a skeleton pattern, or filled in with a mass of stitches.

The colour of the thread makes a difference and should be chosen for its effect. The same colour can look subtle and a contrast can.be dramatic. Flowers can be machined on net or organdie, cut out and applied as a three dimensional effect.

Fabric paint can be used for details of colour.

The flower centre is composed entirely of circles, made from leather, wool and metallic thread, lightly stuck to the background and attached with machine stitches also worked in a circular pattern.

The petals were cut from silk and coarse and fine net. The silk petals were attached all round, but the non-fraying net was only caught at each inner point.

More petal shapes were added as a machine pattern.

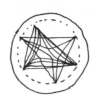

Embroidered buttons

Hand-made buttons add a touch of originality to a garment and buttons can be embroidered on the sewing machine.

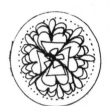

The buttons are based on the metal button shapes, which can be covered with fabric. They are made in several sizes and can be bought at most haberdashers. Read the instructions before beginning.

With sharpened chalk, or paint brush and paint, mark out the circles on cloth stretched taut in an embroidery ring. The outside edge of the fabric will tuck into the back of the button, so the design should be carried out only in the middle of the circle.

The design embroidered depends upon the fabric used, and the garment itself, but it should be very simple. It could be based on a small continuous line motif, or the fabric might be textured with lines of stitching. Try free embroidery with the zigzag, as well as the straight stitch. Contrasting or matching thread could be used, each give a different effect.

If the fabric is fine, back the embroidery with another circle of fabric, so that the metal of the shape does not shine through. Make up by following the manufacturer's instructions.

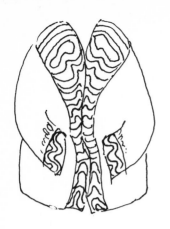

Quilting

English, Italian and trapunto quilting can all be carried out in free machine embroidery. Quilting without the control of the feed dog is never quite as even as ordinary machine quilting. For very regular patterns, therefore, it is quite a good idea to use the foot and feed dog for the straightforward pieces, then use the free machining for the more intricate patterns. For wall hangings and pictures, however, free machining can be used most effectively, but even then it is often easier to carry out any straight lines, using the feed dog. There are several methods of keeping the quilting taut. You have to decide which is most suitable for what you intend to make.

1   An embroidery ring. This is suitable for working small areas of quilting.
2   Mounting on paper-backed fabric. This is useful when the quilting is to be incorporated into a picture or a wall hanging.
3   If one of the layers is stiffened, it is often sufficient to hold the other layers. If the bottom layer is stiff, the wadding and top layer will be held in place. The stiffening can be achieved in several ways: The bottom layer can be dipped in a fabric starch. Use cotton, muslin, scrim or tarletan. The stiffener used for roller blinds is very good. The fabric can also be stiffened with iron-on interfacing, ironed onto the back of the backing, ie top fabric, wadding, interfacing, backing. Both these methods are suitable for clothing.

Free machine embroidery makes it possible to use patterns based on spirals and circles, and these patterns can be used for the various methods of quilting.

It is interesting to experiment with quilting using stretch fabrics (stretch towelling, knitted fabrics) which will accommodate more wadding. Look out for interesting dressmaking fabrics.

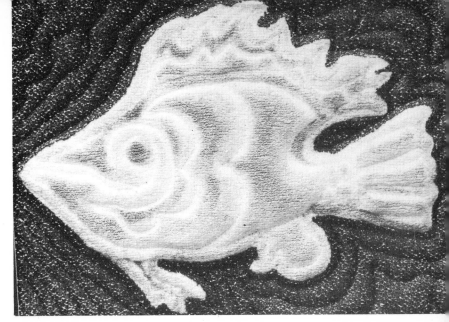

35 Quilted fish decorated with fabric paint

This fish was worked on a piece of light-coloured, knitted fabric. The background is a dark, metallic knit.

Fish make very attractive and often spectacular designs. They have a simple streamlined body shape and lovely colours and patterns. Look out for shapes and colours by noticing fish in aquariums in private houses, in pet shops and garden centres.

To make a quilted fish, you would need:
Stage one
One piece of pale coloured, knitted fabric 20 x 24 cm.
Terylene wadding.
One piece of muslin 24 x 20 cm.
Stage two
One piece of dark, knitted fabric for the background 24 x 20 cm.
Terylene wadding. One piece of stiffened fabric for the base 20 x 24 cm.
Stage one (See diagram on page 116).
1   Transfer the fish pattern onto the light-coloured fabric instructions for transferring patterns on page 22.
2   Put the top layer and the muslin layer in an embroidery ring (20 cm diameter) with three, or four, layers of wadding sandwiched between, but not caught into the ring itself. This means that you can use several layers of wadding (see figure a).
3   Lightly tack the wadding in place behind the design.
4   Make sure both layers are flat.

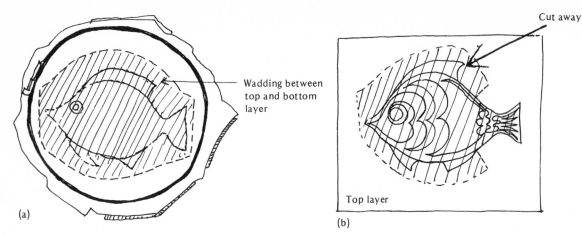

(a)

Wadding between top and bottom layer

Cut away

Top layer

(b)

5   Start sewing in the middle of the design and work outwards. Try to work in a continuous line, even if this means going over some lines twice.

6   Take the materials out of the ring and cut away the wadding and the bottom layer right back to the stitches (figure b). Be careful not to cut through the top layer.

Second stage

1   Choose a piece of stiffened· background fabric.

2   Place two or three layers of terylene wadding on this, then the fish on its background. Pin and tack securely and stitch round the silhouette of the fish.

3   Take the dark background fabric and place over the fish. You now have four layers; dark background, the quilted fish on its background, the wadding, the stiffened backing. Pin and tack these together.

4   Turn to the back of the work, and again stitch round the pattern of the fish.

5   Turn, and you will see the shape of the fish on the top dark layer. Now machine a flowing line pattern over the dark background, round the fish shape.

6   Carefully cut away the background over the fish shape, and reveal the quilted fish which stands out in sharp relief against the dark background.

7   If necessary, colour the fish with fabric paint.

This only gives a small indication of what can be achieved with quilting. One obstacle which might deter you is when the machine refuses to sew through any more layers of wadding, and even then it is easy to push more padding in from the back of the work (see page 46 for trapunto). The machine can work quickly over large areas and by using stiffened fabric as a background, all sorts of exciting results can be achieved, far removed from eiderdowns and anoraks, but using the same basic techniques.

Making faces

Machined faces should be as simple as possible. The smaller the face, the less detail can be included. There are several methods of making faces. The easiest is to cut out an oval and neck of flesh-coloured fabric, and using flesh-coloured thread, machine to the background, indicating the ears with stitches. Features can be sewn by machine or hand. The hair might be an applied fabric shape, or a stitched hair pattern, or both. The face can be made more interesting by adding facial hair, hats and smiles.

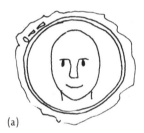

(a)   (b)

Larger faces can be quilted in a small ring. Use flesh-coloured fabric, knitted nylon tights, or cotton. Muslin or tarletan can be used for the bottom layer. Use terylene wadding for padding.

Method one
Machine round the face in flesh-coloured thread, then work the details in a darker thread (figure a). Apply stitch the padded face to the background fabric, and cut back the layers to the stitches. Trim with hair, and so on.

Method two
Machine the facial details, indicating the shape only, with tacking stitches (figure b). Cut a piece of card the same size as the head. Lightly glue to the backing. Cut the wadding and backing to the edge of the card, leaving the top layer intact. Pull the top layer round the card. This head shape can be trimmed, and stands free.
When making quilted faces, make the nose an enclosed space, so that you can push in more wadding from the back, to make the nose stand out.

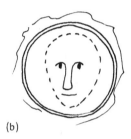

36 Flower on white linen, the edges finished with zigzag

Cut work

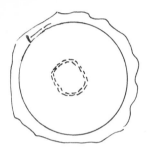

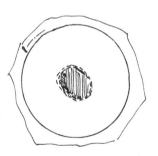

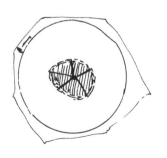

In hand embroidery, cut work is usually carried out in buttonhole stitch, enclosing areas which are then cut out and decorated with buttonholed bars. It has a lacy quality which is very attractive. A sewing machine cannot do buttonhole stitch, so cut work is usually carried out in straight stitch, or zigzag satin stitch, in some cases. The work can be carried out on firmly woven fabric, like linen, linen-type dress fabrics, organdie, net and even leather or suede. Cut work looks attractive on clothes when worked on fabric with matching thread. To practise, use felt which is easy to manage and will not fray. Put the work in a small frame to keep taut. Use an embroidery or darning foot, or no foot at all. Normal tension.

Make a ring of straight stitches, going round the circle two or three times. Cut the middle out of the circle, being careful not to cut the stitches themselves.

Using straight stitch, run the machine from one side of the hole to the other. As the machine goes across the space, the top and bottom threads will twist together to from a bar.

Take the machine smoothly across the space several times to make a spider's web, taking care to move the ring gently and not to pull at the threads, and thus bend the needle.

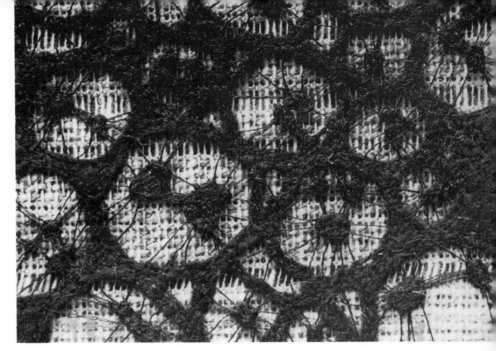

37 Felt is an easy fabric to use as it does not fray

The edges of the holes can be finished off with a close zigzag, but this is only necessary for articles which will need laundering.

Thus a whole area of fabric can be patterned with spaces decorated with bars.

Always stitch round each space two or three times before cutting out, to maintain the tension, and also to give the bars an anchor. Only cut and decorate one space at a time, before moving on to the next.

It is possible to work out various bar patterns, and bars can be decorated with pips, which are made by going round and round an intersection with machine stitches.

Designs for this technique should have a simple outline shape, and be patterned with interesting spaces, which are cut out and decorated. Do not attempt very big spaces, but try to give variety with square and round spaces and various bar combinations. The finished work can be mounted over a contrasting coloured fabric.

This technique can also be used on leather and suede, which are stiff enough to hold in shape without a ring.

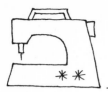

Loosely woven fabrics

These fabrics can be used to make interesting patterns, textures and motifs which can be used in various ways.

The fabric must be kept taut in a ring.

Suitable fabric includes all types of scrim, tarletan, muslin, some curtain fabrics.

First method using zigzag stitch
To practise, use tarletan, with the weft and warp running straight.

(a) Set the machine at medium width zigzag. Work a line of zigzag stitches down the fabric. With sharp scissors, cut the fabric next to the stitches, taking care not to cut the stitches themselves.

(b) Cover the raw edge made with zigzag stitches. Pull fabric taut again.

(c) and (d) Keep cutting the fabric next to the stitches, then stitching the raw edges. This gives a pattern of lines, which might be turned into a motif.

38 This motif was worked on tartletan, cut out and mounted onto a background fabric and attached with satin stitch

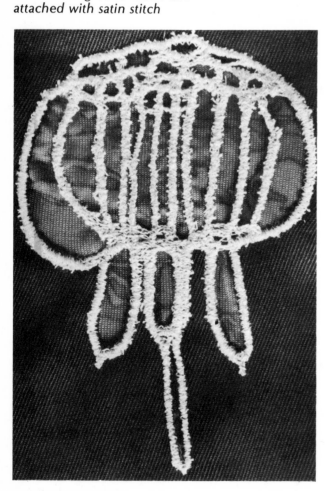

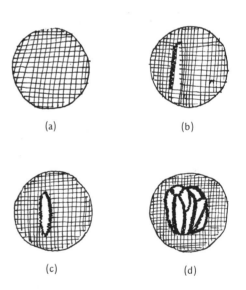

(a) (b)

(c) (d)

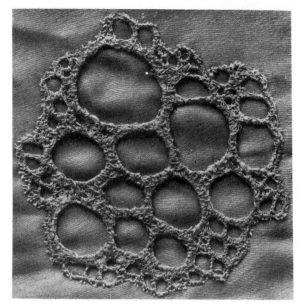

39 *A textured motif worked on linen scrim*

Second method with straight stitch or zigzag

(a) Stretch a piece of scrim in a ring.

(b) With your finger, poke a hole in the fabric, and stretch the fabric as much as possible without tearing the threads.

(c) With straight stitch, moving the work from side to side while sewing, or with zigzag stitch, bind the edge of the hole. Drive the machine slowly, and pull the fabric quickly.

(d) and (e) Keep poking holes in the fabric and binding the edges. As the work progresses, more holes will appear round the edge of the work. Bind these also and make an attractive textured fabric.

These textures can be executed in a simple shape, and used as motifs on clothing. They can be attached by mounting the shape on the chosen background, and going round the edge in close satin stitch, using a matching thread. Cut the surplus fabric back to the stitches. The motif might need one or two stitches in the middle to hold it in place.

Experiment on various loosely woven fabrics to see the effect created.

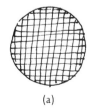 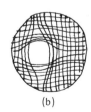 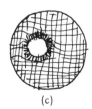 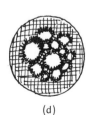 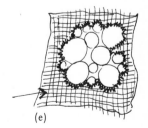

(a) (b) (c) (d) (e)

Removing threads

A fabric can be changed completely by cutting holes in it and by pulling holes in it, and decorating the edges and the spaces. It is also possible to create a texture by removing some threads from a fabric and decorating the spaces thus created.

Many fabrics are woven loosely enough to remove threads. Choose an evenly woven fabric like linen, hessian, various scrims, many modern curtain fabrics and even some loosely woven tweeds and dress fabrics. Test the fabric before embarking on a project, for some fabrics are deceptive and instead of the threads pulling out smoothly, they get caught up and disintegrate.

Method one

Threads can be pulled right out of a piece of fabric in a formal pattern, either across, or down, or both. The square, or oblong section to be decorated should fit within the embroidery ring. Leave plenty of spare fabric round the edge.

Use a zigzag stitch and oversew the threads into groups. Some threads can be left undecorated. The spaces might be decorated with bars or spider's webs. This sort of work looks attractive when mounted over a contrasting fabric, but it gives a very rich texture if the fabric, thread and backing fabric, are all the same colour. The piece of rectangular textured fabric created might be used as a patch of decoration on a pocket or a bag.

Opposite

The hippy *Machine* embroidery on fabric appliqué. The picture was inspired by a group of London buskers seen after visiting the Victorian and Albert Museum to see the miniatures of Nicholas Hilliard

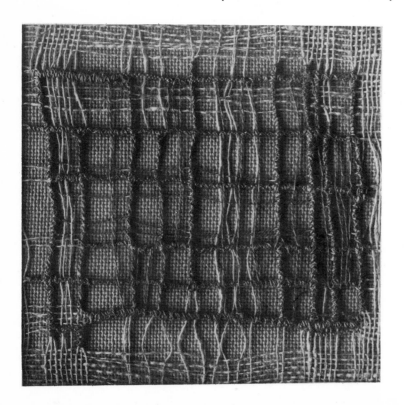

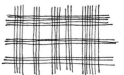

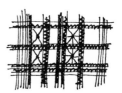

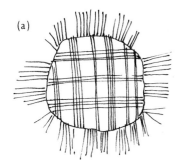

(a)

Opposite

A machine can be used to decorate both garments and household articles. The shawl is decorated with flowers, free machined on velvet, cut out and applied. The tree on the waistcoat was worked in close zigzag and the bird shapes were decorated with free machining and white fabric paint

Cushions

1 English quilting on satin using straight stitch

2 Log cabin patchwork, using strips of corduroy

3 and 4 Felt shapes applied to a felt background and machine stitched

5 Patchwork made from triangles cut from striped fabric

6 Strips of fabric in different widths joined to make an area of cloth

Second method

Threads can be pulled out within a shape, then darned back into the edges of the fabric.

With chalk, draw a simple shape on a piece of loosely woven fabric. Make a slit in the centre and pull out the threads up to the chalk line, both weft and warp, leaving some threads to make a grid across the hole (see figure a).

The threads can be darned back into the fabric with a needle, or as in the photograph, twisted into coils, pinned, or lightly glued, then couched down with machine stitches worked in a spiral pattern. The warp and weft threads across the centre are then bound with stitches, either with a zigzag, or a straight stitch, moving the frame from side to side when stitching.

The intersections can be decorated with pips, taking the machine round and round each intersection as illustrated above: In this sample, the machining was done with the bottom tension slightly loosened (see page 107 for details of how to do this).

97

Nets

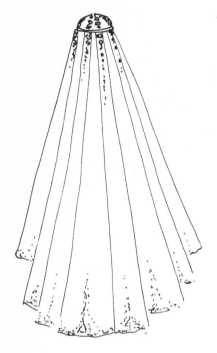

Over the last few pages, we have been looking at ways in which different and interesting textures can be created by making holes in fabric. There is a group of materials which are constructed so that they are already full of holes. These are net materials and range from fine tulle, through curtain nets, to knitted and crocheted nets, vegetable net and even plastic wire netting. All of these can be used as a basis for machine embroidery, and although not all can be put to any practical use, they are very interesting to work and can sometimes be incorporated into wall hangings. Some are suitable for decoration of dress and accessories.

Tulle

This fabric is made from silk or nylon. It is good tempered and easy to manage, in spite of its fragile appearance. Hold the net taut in a ring. With straight stitch, or zigzag, machine patterns on the net just as if it was an ordinary fabric.

Because the net is semi-transparent, it is easy to sew a picture or pattern onto it by tacking the design traced onto tissue paper to the underside of the net, so that it can be seen through the fabric. Whenever you are sewing through any design in this way, go over only the main lines of the pattern, then tear off the paper and fill in all the details freehand. Little pieces of paper can become caught in a dense mass of machine embroidery and can be very difficult to remove.

42 Black embroidery on black net

Work can be mounted over contrasting fabric, so that the patterns can be seen clearly. A background can even be painted on fabric, with fabric paint. Make use of the transparency of the net to make a picture, or hanging for a window, so that the light can shine through and show up the patterns. This sort of hanging can be mounted on a piece of wooden dowelling.

A more complicated arrangement can be made, using several layers of embroidered net, mounted onto cardboard or thin wooden frames and set one behind the other to give a three dimensional window picture.

Tulle is manufactured in various colours. Black on black looks very dramatic, and white on white looks beautiful, but there is no reason why several layers of coloured net should not be used, superimposed, sewn and cut away in reverse appliqué.

It is really worthwhile buying a packet of different net squares to experiment, for it is such an interesting and easy fabric to handle. Tulle is used for making special clothes, particularly bridal veils and dance dresses. Try to do the embroidery before cutting the fabric. However, this might be difficult where you have to embroider right up to the edge of the fabric. Tack a strip of interfacing to the edge of the net, overlapping by about 1 cm. This will go into an embroidery ring and help to hold the net taut. It can be removed when the work is finished.

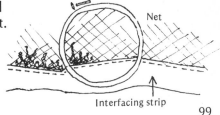

Net

Interfacing strip

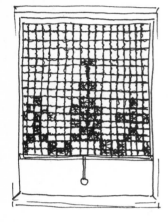

Occasionally it is possible to buy quite substantial wide mesh curtaining, woven in diamond, or square mesh, with no decoration. Cotton and cotton mixes are easier to manage than nylon.

The net is held taut in a frame and the diamond, or square mesh is decorated with a pattern, based on either one square, or a group of squares. Thread can either match or contrast with the net. Patterns can be worked out first on paper. Consider dyeing the net to a suitable colour either before, or after it has been worked.

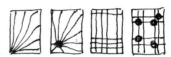

Alternatively, a mesh can be crocheted. This pattern is for a square mesh net. The bigger the hook, the thicker the thread, the larger the mesh.

Make 8 chain plus any multiple of 3 (eg 26, or 29, or 38 etc). To practise, use a medium hook and crochet cotton.

Make 32 chain.

1st row. Work one treble into 8th. chain from hook. (ch. on hook counts as one) *2ch., miss next 2ch., 1tr. into next ch. Repeat from * to end.

2nd. row. Turn with 5ch. Miss 1st. ch. space, 1tr. into next tr., *2ch., miss next 2 ch. space, 1 tr. into next treble. Repeat from 1* to end, finishing with 1tr. into 3rd. ch. of the turning chain.

Repeat 2nd row for pattern.

43Machine embroidery on crochet net

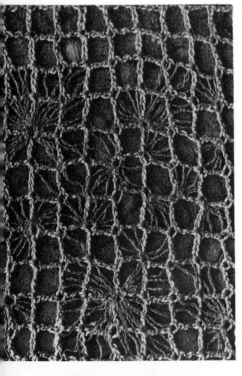

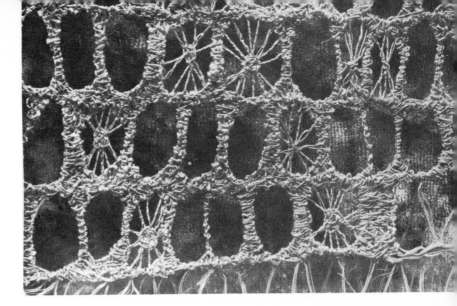

Plastic net

There are various types of plastic net used to hold vegetables and fruit, and these can often be used quite successfully, as the basis for a machined pattern.

The nets must be held taut in a ring and are worked in the same way as ordinary mesh. The easiest to use are the nets used for potato bags, made from fairly soft plastic raffia. The more rigid plastic nets are slightly more difficult in that the needle occasionally hits the plastic, which it cannot pierce. The plastic is pushed into the throat plate and makes the machine splutter out a few inches of extra cotton. You can either machine this into a pip, or cut the cotton and start again.

This sort of work is really experimental, but the cotton nets and the crochet net produce square or rectangular pieces of embroidered material, which might be incorporated into an article as an insertion, or be

44 Machine embroidery on plastic rafia mesh (vegetable net)

45 Machine embroidery on plastic netting

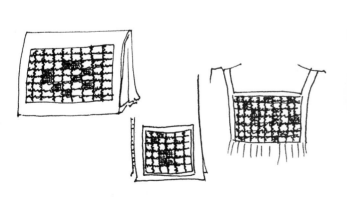

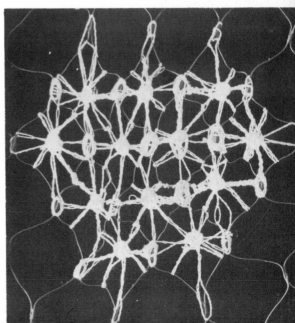

mounted as a decorative panel. Even vegetable nets can sometimes be turned into a surprisingly attractive fabric, for the plastic colour is considerably toned down by the thread. It is a good idea to choose a colour to tone in with the colour of the net. All these heavy types of mesh combine well with materials like leather, suede and PVC, as well as more ordinary, heavy fabrics.

Embroidering on plastic net
Clematis net is one of the thicker garden nets. Because it is rigid, the square grid can be used as a basis for making patterns with the machine.

The crossbars can be bound with thread by moving the net from side to side while sewing, driving the machine slowly and steadily. The cross bars are bound a few cm at a time, then the thread is taken across to the other side and another part of the crossbar is bound. Gradually, the whole net can be covered using two or three colours, and making bars crisscrossing the spaces between the crossbars. The pips are made by stitching round and round the intersections of the bars. These are made more interesting by stitching round several times with different coloured threads.

46 Machine embroidery on clematis net

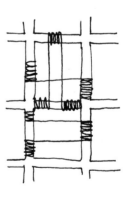

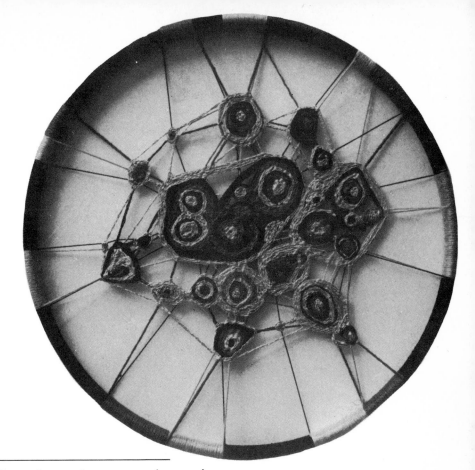

Making a circular hanging

Wooden rings, or small, firm picture frames can be made into effective decorations. The edge of the ring is first bound by hand, using several colours. Red, cream and black were used in this case. The thread used should be fairly strong, and crochet cotton, or knitting cotton are most suitable.

Now and again, the binding thread is taken across the ring, so that a network of taut threads crisscrosses the middle.

The machining is started at an intersection. Hold both threads in one hand as is usual when starting to machine embroider. After a few stitches, cut the threads, and the ends will be lost in the mass of stitches. Little islands are formed by going round and round, then moving to another intersection and so on.

Using the three colours, one at a time, the islands are gradually enlarged and eventually joined up.

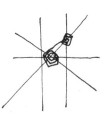
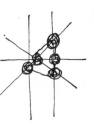

Covering wire with thread

This is an easy way of covering wire with thread, so that it can be incorporated into a piece of embroidery where a three-dimensional effect might be needed.

Use plastic-coated garden wire.

The machine is set at 2.5-3 mm zigzag, so that the stitch takes in the wire, without being too loose.

Use an ordinary foot, and use the feed dog, which helps to hold the wire. First cover the wire with a fairly open zigzag, then go over it again with a satin stitch. It is much easier to start in the centre and machine out to the end of the wire, then come back to the middle and out to the other end of the wire, come back and finish in the centre, so that the end threads are all in the middle and cannot ravel off the ends. Leave a tiny piece of wire at each end, which can be turned back over the stitches with a pair of pliers to stop the stitches coming off.

48 The petal spaces have also been machine embroidered and decorated

Stiffening fabrics for machine embroidery with cellulose paste

Cellulose or wallpaper paste can be used to prepare a fabric for machine embroidery. The paste is mixed according to the directions on the packet. The fabric is dipped into the paste and the excess paste is squeezed out. The fabric is then spread out to dry thoroughly. It is best to experiment with small pieces of a variety of fabrics, because the results are much more satisfactory with some fabrics than with others, and do not show a residue of glue.

Try tarletan, scrim, hessian, muslin and cotton.

The fabric can be used either as a base for appliqué, or as a basis for practising machine embroidered patterns.

However, the soaked fabric can also be pushed into folds and pleats or pulled into holes and spaces while still wet. It can then be left to dry thoroughly. The resulting three-dimensional shape can be further adorned with lines of stitches and spiderwebs.

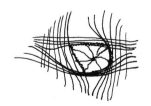

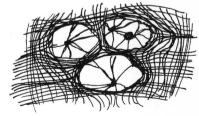

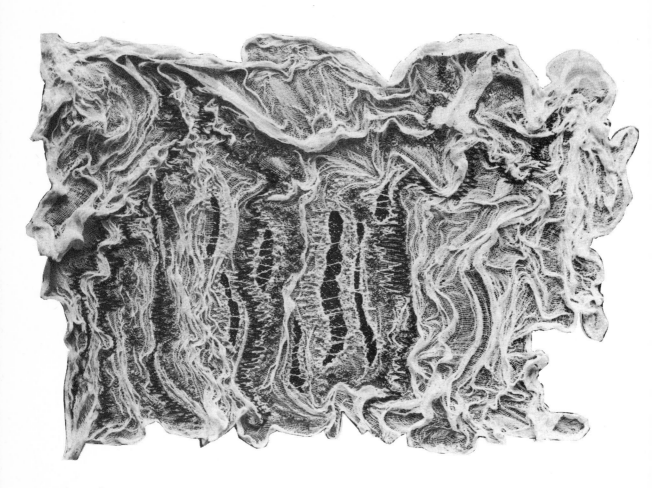

49 Three dimensional shape made from tarletan, decorated with lines of machine embroidery

Use a thick machine needle and no foot. Embroider in the spaces between folds, and across the gaps and holes. Mount over interesting and decorative fabrics like satin, brocade, metallic fabric, so as to shine through the spaces.

The bobbin

Look now at the bobbin, in the bobbin case. The thread wound onto the bobbin is threaded under a steel spring in the bobbin case, which keeps the thread at the correct tension. The spring is controlled by a screw. All sewing machines are designed in a similar way, although the shape of the bobbin, or spool and the bobbin case, may vary.

Take the bobbin case, with the bobbin in it, out of the machine. Make sure the thread is passing through the spring and gently pull the thread. You will see that it moves smoothly in a controlled manner, not too slack and not too tight.

If you hold the end of the thread and let the bobbin and case hang in mid-air, the thread should just hold them without the thread running through. The bobbin and case should only move if you give the thread a little jerk.

All this is important as you should know how to feel the correct tension on the bobbin in your machine, so that you can alter it if necessary, then adjust it back to the correct tension for dressmaking. Look at the screw which controls the spring. Make a written note of the angle of the thread on the top of the screw. Write it down so that you will remember it.

With the screwdriver provided with your machine, loosen the screw one revolution (ie 360°).

Turn anticlockwise to loosen. Turn clockwise to tighten.

Set the machine for embroidery in the same way as usual, with an embroidery foot and no feed dog. Practising on a scrap of stiffened fabric, or fabric in a ring, start to sew.

50 Free machine embroidery on applied fabric. The fleeces are worked in tight spirals with the bobbin tension loosened to create a raised line

You will see that the loosened tension causes the bottom thread to loop up so that it makes a thick corded line on top of the fabric. When you have finished the work, remove the bobbin and case and tighten the screw back to where it was, this time turning clockwise one revolution.

Check to see that it sews with correct tension. Gradually, by frequent checking of the tension, both by feeling and looking and by making a note of the position of the screw and the number of revolutions it has been turned, you become familiar with the bobbin, and can alter the tension quite easily.

Textures using tension variations

In some machines, you can get a similar effect by bypassing the tension spring altogether, and threading the bottom thread through any convenient gap next to the tension spring. However, this gives no control over the size of the loops pulled through and they will all be uniformly large. It is a good idea to try this method too.

A loosened bottom tension gives a very attractive texture. Try making tightly curved patterns which make the loops go into tight little flower-like structures. Make curved line patterns and see how the loops are pulled from side to side.

Variations can be made by driving the machine slowly and pulling the fabric quickly through the machine, or by driving quickly and taking the fabric through slowly. Always drive smoothly.

Try this technique on various fabrics like organdie, net, satin, and try graduated machine embroidery threads wound on the bobbin. With zigzag, another texture is created.

It is possible to make a tufted texture by carefully removing the top thread and leaving the loops sticking through the fabric. It is easier to do this using a contrasting top thread, which can be seen and pulled out. Be careful not to pull the bottom thread. Immediately, iron interfacing to the back of the work to lock the loops in position. This can also be done with a zigzag stitch, making parallel lines of loops. Some machines have a basting foot, to make tailor's tacks, and this also makes a tufted texture.

51 A tufted texture is achieved by removing the top thread

Winding thicker threads on the bobbin
Crochet cotton, or fine wool can be wound round the bobbin by hand, so that when machined, the thicker thread is couched onto the underside of the fabric.

The thread should be wound firmly and evenly onto the bobbin, and threaded through the tension spring. Loosen the screw so that the thicker thread will pull through evenly. Practise on stiffened fabric, working on the back of the fabric and not the front. If the material is held in a ring, make sure the front of the fabric faces the base of the machine.

Work in exactly the same way as for free embroidery, being particularly careful to bring both threads to the top before beginning. The design to be followed can be marked out on the back of the fabric.
You can use any smooth thread which will pass through the tension spring.

53 Automatic patterns look
attractive worked in a
circle (see page 113)

Automatic patterns

It is possible to make a wide variety of patterns with an ordinary sewing machine. Some modern machines have automatic stitch patterns incorporated and these make use of cams to make patterns (see page 10).

These patterns are absolutely regular and for this reason, many people find them dull. However, it is a pity not to make use of every gadget and stitch available and to experiment with the stitches to see what they will do and how they can be used for decoration.

From the machine manual, find out how to work the automatic patterns. Patterns can be changed both in density of stitch and width of stitch, just as zigzag patterns can. The patterns usually look best when worked on the widest setting, but quite considerable changes can be made by altering the density of the stitches. They look completely different worked in satin stitch from when they are worked spaced apart. Try every pattern on a length of firmly woven fabric. Keep the patterns for reference.

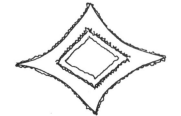

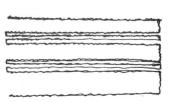

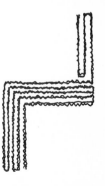

Automatic patterns are worked with an ordinary foot and the feed dog controlling the fabric. The top tension may need loosening slightly, as in zigzag stitch. The patterns can be used in the same way as straight stitch and zigzag to make line patterns and motifs, made from continuous straight and slightly curved lines.

Make use of a wide variety of fabrics. Automatic patterns can look really pretty on striped fabric, gingham and checks, as well as spotted and regularly printed fabrics.

Organdie, satin, ribbon voile and other delicate fabrics can be decorated with lines and blocks of pattern, either in contrasting or matching thread. Although the patterns are regular, the length of the line does not have to be, and some lines can be long, some short.

Some stitches can be used to bridge two edges together, like faggoting and some stitches make a fancy satin stitch which can be used as an edging. Cut the fabric back to the stitches.

The automatic patterns can be used to attach fabric in appliqué and also to sew on braids, ribbons, bindings and lace. Use either matching, or contrasting thread.

Patterns are ideal for making crazy patchwork. Take a piece of plain cotton, or calico, for a background. Cut pieces of cotton fabric into shapes with straight sides. You can use any firmly woven fabric including velvet and corduroy, but the whole patchwork must be made of the same type of fabric. Start at one edge and pin two patches onto the background, one overlapping the other. There is no need to turn in the edge. Sew down the overlapping edge, choosing one of the patterns. Keep adding patches one by one, overlapping and sewing. Use the same pattern throughout. Try to keep a balance between light and dark fabrics.

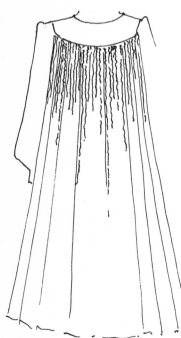

Circular sewing

A circle is a simple and satisfying shape. Sewing a circle is quite easy on any sewing machine.

Take an embroidery ring about 26 cm diameter and stretch a piece of firmly woven fabric in it. Find the centre (approximately) and stick a piece of tape (only 2 or 3 cm) across the middle. This will stop the fabric from stretching into a big hole.

Some machines are bedded into a table which is on the same level as the throat plate and some have an extension table which is also on the same level as the throat plate. In these cases, take a drawing pin, and tape it to the base, about 10 cm to the left of the needle, point upwards. It must be held absolutely still (see figure a).

Put the ring under the needle, with the drawing pin sticking up through the centre of the fabric, through the piece of tape. Use an ordinary foot, the feed dog should be in control. Machine, and the ring will go round the drawing pin, which acts as a pivot. Just hold the drawing pin lightly, in case it moves (see figure b)

By moving the drawing pin from place to place, it is possible to make bigger circles, 7 cm is about the smallest possible.

If the machine is standing above the table, take a block of wood the same height as the throat plate and attach a drawing pin to that in the same way. The block can be stuck to the table either with a sucker, or plastic gum, and moved when necessary. (see figure c).

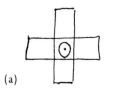

(a)

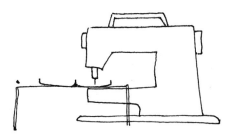

(b)

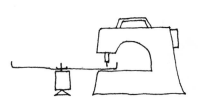

(c)

Circles can be used in quilting, or with a twin needle. Automatic patterns look lovely worked in a circle, particularly black on white (see page 111). Circles can be used to decorate clothes and accessories, as well as home furnishings like cushions, table-mats and curtains. The shapes can be mounted over card and used as a frame for a piece of embroidery, pressed flowers, or even a photograph. Straight stitches and zigzag stitches can be used, and decorated with fabric paint to add interest.

Most of the ideas in this book come from using the basic sewing machine with a variety of materials. Machines often have gadgets which can be used to produce even more different and exciting effects. A sewing machine is only a tool. You are the operator and it is only through you that the machine can be explored, exploited and used in a truly creative way.

Suppliers in Great Britain

C and F Handicraft (Supplies) Ltd
346 Stag Lane, Kingsbury, London NW9 9AG
*DMC gold and silver thread for the bobbin, and machine
embroidery cotton. Supplied through stockists; the firm will
put you in touch with the nearest stockist*

Fred Aldous Handicrafts
37 Lever Street, Manchester M60 1UX
Frames, special fabrics etc

MacCulloch & Wallis Ltd
25/26 Dering Street, London W1R 0BH
Various types of machine embroidery cottons

Nottingham Handcraft Limited
17 Ludlow Hill Road
Melton Road, West Bridgford, Nottingham NG2 6HD
Frames, special fabrics etc

Silken Strands
31 Park Crescent, Furness Vale, Stockport SK12 7PU
Capstan machine embroidery thread

Stephen Simpson Ltd
Avenham Works, Preston PR1 3UR
*Fine Lurex silver and gold as a top thread. Will supply direct to
the public*

J Henry Smith Ltd
Park Road, Calverton, Nottingham NG14 6LL
*Machine embroidery thread No. 30, and gold and silver machine
thread. Will supply direct to the public*

Filmstrips on embroidery by Anne Coleman are obtainable
from Focal Point Filmstrips, 251 Copnor Road, Portsmouth PO3 5EE
Entitled 'Fun with Machine Embroidery' the filmstrip is in two
parts:
Part 1 Controlled Embroidery
Part 2 Free Embroidery

Suppliers in the USA

Threads and embroidery accessories

American Thread Corporation
90 Park Avenue, New York

Bucky King Embroideries Unlimited
121 South Drive, Pittsburgh Pennsylvania 15238

The Rusty Needle
1479 Glenneyre, Laguna Beach, California 92651

Joan Toggitt
1170 Broadway, New York, NY 10001

Yarn Depot
545 Sutter Street, San Francisco 95102

Further Reading

Designs for Machine Embroidery, Ira Lillow
Enjoying Embroidery, Anna Wilson
Inspiration for Embroidery, Constance Howard
Introducing Design in Embroidery, Betty Chicken
Machine Embroidery: Technique and Design, Jennifer Gray
Machine Stitchery, Gay Swift
Machine Stitches, Anne Butler
Colour and Embroidery, Constance Howard
Design in Embroidery, Kathleen Whyte

All published by Batsford, London

Index

Main page references are in *italic* type

Accessories, (see under Decoration)
Appliqué, 17, *25-28*, 53, 57, 63, 65, 66, 67, *68-70*, *76-81*, 85, 86, 108, colour facing pages 73, 96, 97; background for *26-27*, 28, 57, 63, *64-66*, *77-79*; reverse appliqué 28, *58-59*, 83, 84
Automatic patterns 10, 11, 15, *112-113*, 114

Background (see under Appliqué, Felt, Firmly woven fabric, Loose woven fabric, Net, Organdie, Paper-backed fabric, Even weave fabric)
Binding 19, 38
Bobbin 9, 10, *13*, 63, *107-108*, *109*; thick threads for *110*
Bonding web (see under Interfacing)
Braids 38
Buttons embroidered *87*
Brocade 16, 58, 68, 106

Cams *10*, 111
Calico 26, 45, 54
Chain stitch machine 9
Cheesecloth 42
Chiffon 16, 17, 45, 47, 53, 58, 77, 79
Circular sewing *113-114*
Clothes (see under Decoration)
Colour *29-31*;
   complementary 31; contrasting 85;
   experiments with fabrics 29-31;
   hues 30; in appliqué 77;
   mixing 29; primary 29;
   tones 30; with texture *52-53*; wheel 29
Cord 45, 51, 61
Corduroy 17, 32, 33, 77, 112
Cotton, crochet 38, 40, 100, 103, 110;
   fabric 16, *32*, *33*, 49, 50, 52, *58-59*, 60, 84;
   as background 17, 42, *54*, 63, 88, 105;
   knitting 38, 40, 103; thread *13*
Couching *38*, *91*
Crêpe 45
Cut work 60, *92-93*

Darning foot *64*, 65, 66, 82, 92
Discs *10*
Decoration, suitable for accessories,
   clothes and soft furnishings *18-22*,
   27, 28, *32-37*, 38, 40, *41-47*, *50-51*, *57-63*, 66-69,
   82-85, 87, 88, *92-97*, *98-101*, *109-114*
Denim 18

Design, block and grid patterns *41*, *43*; (see also Patchwork) 47, 96, 97, 100, 101, 102; geometric shapes *25-27*, 70, 79, *83-86*, 88, 113; human face and form *80-81*, *91*; linear and border patterns *18-19*, 45, 46, 56, 60, 67, 70, *111-112*; maze patterns 61; motifs *20-21*, 31, 44, *56-59*, 60, 67, 87, 93, 94, 95, *111-112*; on circles 28; natural forms *68*, *85*, *86*, *89*; photographs *25-26*, 73, 76; representational pictures *71-76*; three dimensional forms 102, *103*, *104*, *105-106*; using texture *52-53*
Double top thread 13, 18
Dupion 17, 77, 79

Embroidery ring 22, 63, 65, 68, *82-85*, 87, 110;
   for circular sewing 113; for cut work 92;
   for loose woven fabric 94-97; for quilting 88, 89, 90, 91; with net 99-101
Enlarging and reducing a design *24*
Even weave fabric 56

Fabric (see *also* under specific names)
   collection *16*, 76;
   grouping *17*; stiffener 88
   storage *17*; strips 30, *32-33*, 38, 40, 77, 79
Feed dog 9, 10, 64, 66, 82, 88, 104, 107, 112, 113
Felt 28, 38, 47; as background *92-93*,
   colour facing page 97
Finishing off *14*
Firmly woven fabric 45, 112
   as background 17, 18, 26, 28, 47, 92
Fringe *38*, 39, 61, 67, colour facing page 72

Georgette 79
Gold lamé 17
Glue, cellulose paste 66, *105-106*;
   fabric 26, 47, 68, 69, 78, 79, 86, 97;
   PVA *65*; plastic gum 113; sticky tape 22, 57, 113

Hessian 52, 105
Home furnishings (see under Decoration)
Human figures (see under Design)

Ironing and pressing 17, 22, 27, 33, 37, 44
Interfacing 99; bonding web 26, *54*, 57, 59, 63;
   iron-on 26, 54, 57, 63, 66, 68, 88

Knitted fabric 12, 17, 28, 49, 52, 88, *89-90*

Lace 16, 17, 38
Lawn 50, 60
Leather and suede *12*, 14, 16, 17, 22, 28, 38, 47, *57*, 92, 102
Linen 92

Loose woven fabric 40, 46, 94;
  as background 94-97, 105-106

Machine embroidery thread 13, 54, 63
Machine types 15
Metallic thread 38, 40, 86
Muslin 94; as backing 42, 45, 46 49, 63, 88, 89, 105

Needle 9, 10, 12, 61, 66, 78, 92, 101, 106;
  leather 12, 57; needle bar 9, 10, 11, 12;
  threading 12; twin needle 45, 114
Net 16, 17, 52, 53, 58, 77, 83, 86, 92;
  as background 83, 98-102, 109;
  crochet 100; plastic 16, 101-102; tulle 98-99
Non-fray fabric 28, 38, 47, 58
Nylon 12, 17, 42, 45; knit 46, 49, 91

Organdie 17, 45, 47, 58, 60, 84, 92, 109
  as background 60, 109

Padding 39, 41, 42; with foam 42, 49;
  with kapok 46;
  with shredded tights 46, 49, 91;
  with wadding 42, 44, 46, 49, 88, 89, 90, 91
Paper-backed fabric 65, 66, 68, 70, 78, 88, 90,
  colour facing page 73
Patchwork, crazy 112;
  diamonds 37; leather and suede 57;
  log cabin 33; pleated squares 50;
  squares 36; strips 32; triangles 36,
  colour facing page 97;
  templates 34, 35
Pattern (see under Design)
Patterned fabric 17, 19, 26, 27, 31, 32, 33, 44, 49, 51, 59,
  70, 81, 112
Pictures (see under Wall hangings)
Pinning and tacking 14, 21, 22, 26, 32, 33, 36, 44, 49, 57,
  68, 69, 79, 90, 99, 112
Pips and bars 92, 96, 97, 100, 102, 103
Pleating 50-51, 52, 105
Presser foot 9
Preventing accidents 12
Program 11
Polyester cotton 42, 45, 49, 60;
  thread 13
Polystyrene 49
Polythene 14
PVC 14, 38, 47, 101

Quilting 41-49, 52, 88-91;
  design for 43-44; english 42, 114,
  colour facing page 97;
  italian 45; shadow 47;
  trapunto 46, 90; wool 45, 51

Rayon 58
Ribbon 19, 38

Sailcloth 17, 18
Satin 16, 17, 38, 42, 45, 47, 50-51, 53, 58, 68, 77, 79, 84,
  106, 109, 112;
  stitch (close zigzag) 55, 57, 58, 59, 60, 61, 104;
  graduated width 62-63
Sewing machine, history 7-9;
  how it works 9-11; preparation for use 12-13;
  preventing accidents 12;
  hand-operated, treadle, zigzag
  (see under straight stitch machine)
Scrim 40, 42, 45, 46, 88, 94-97, 105
Silk 32, 45, 58, 68, 86
Spider's web 92, 96, 103, 105
String 45, 61
Stitch ripper 14
Straight stitch machine
  hand-operated 9, 15, 18; uses 25-53, 113-114;
  foot-operated (treadle) 15-18;
  uses 25-53, 64-93, 95, 97, 98-103, 105-110, 113-114,
  colour facing page 97
Stretch fabric 42, 46, 52, 88

Taffeta 45, 52, 68
Tacking (see under Pinning)
Taking out 14
Tarletan 46, 88, 94, 99, 105
Tension 82, 92, 93;
  bottom 13, 97, 107-110;
  top 12, 18, 54, 63, 65, 77, 95, 107-109
Textures 38-40, 41, 51, 52-53, 65, 77, 95, 107-109
Threads 9,13 (see also under specific names)
Throat plate 64, 101, 113
Top stitch thread 13
Transferring designs 21, 22-23, 25-26, 49, 68, 78;
  for couching 38, 61; for quilting 44
Trevira 17, 18
Tweed 16, 17, 33, 52, 77, 96

Vanishing muslin 66
Velvet 16, 17, 32, 33, 58, 112
Voile 50, 60, 112

Wall hangings and pictures 25-28, 38, 39, 40, 42, 49, 50,
  52-53, 58-59, 62-63, 65-70, 77-81, 86, 88, 89-90, 91,
  98-99, 100-103, 104, 105-106, 108, 114;
  composition and arrangement 74-75, 76;
  details 76; final plan 76;
  keeping records 72-73; looking for ideas 71-76;
  using simple shapes 76, 79, 81
Weaving yarn 38, 40
Wire, covering with thread 104
Wool, fabric 17, 38, 58; thread 38, 40, 45, 51, 53, 61, 86,
  110; rug 38, 40

Zigzag machine 9, 10, 11, 15, 18;
  attachment 11, 15; covering wire 104;
  graduated stitch width 54, 62;
  stitch density 54;
  specific use 54-63;
  general use 25-110, 113-114, colour facing page 97